near and true

The Minor Prophets Speak to Your Life Today

a devotional look at the Minor Prophets

By David Guzik

The grass withers, the flower fades,
but the word of our God stands forever.
Isaiah 40:8

Near and True
Copyright ©2019 by David Guzik
ISBN 1-56599-032-3
Printed in the United States of America
or in the United Kingdom

Enduring Word

5662 Calle Real #184

Goleta, CA 93117

Electronic Mail: ewm@enduringword.com

Internet Home Page: www.enduringword.com

Cover photograph by Craig Brewer ©2005
www.craigbrewer.com

Scripture references, unless noted, are from the New King James Version of the Bible, copyright © 1979, 1980, 1982, Thomas Nelson, Inc., Publisher.

**Dedicated to
Nick and Sue Long,
precious among
God's servants
and our friends**

A FEW WORDS FROM THE AUTHOR

The Minor Prophets are called "minor," not because they are less important but simply because their books are smaller than the "major" prophets such as Isaiah, Ezekiel, and Jeremiah. These 13 books are a commonly negelected part of the Bible. Yet the message of these obscure men, speaking to their distant times, echoes across the ages to today.

These prophets did not all speak in the same century, or to the same people, from the same life backgrounds, or from the same places. Yet since they all spoke as representatives of the true God, they spoke with a common voice. They emphasized the idea that God wants a *near* and a *true* relationship with man. There is a wonderful emphasis on *relationship* in these 13 books that can be a blessing for any seeker of God.

David Guzik
December 2005
Siegen, Germany

ONE
Bible Reading: Hosea 1

THREE STRANGE NAMES

Now when she had weaned Lo-Ruhamah, she conceived and bore a son. Then God said: "Call his name Lo-Ammi, for you are not My people, and I will not be your God." (Hosea 1:8-9)

Hosea the Prophet had a unique and difficult job - God told him to marry a prostitute as a way to illustrate the relationship between God and His people. When they married, his wife (named Gomer) didn't give up her prior profession. Because of his cheating wife, Hosea had a unique perspective on how God *felt* about cheating Israel, who didn't faithfully love God the way that God loved them.

In the course of time three children were born to this unhappy family, and each child is mentioned in Hosea 1. The first son was named "**Jezreel**" and his name spoke of two things. First, **Jezreel** means "Scattered," and Israel would soon be scattered in exile by the Assyrians. Second, **Jezreel** refers to the Valley of Jezreel, where Jehu - the founder of the dynasty that currently ruled Israel - massacred all the descendants of the previous dynasty, thus establishing his throne (2 Kings 10:11). God directed Hosea to name his son **Jezreel** to confirm His promise to avenge the bloodshed of Jezreel by judging the house of Jehu.

The second baby was a girl, and named **Lo-Ruhamah**. Her name meant "No Mercy." Every call to this child with the unfortunate name reminded Hosea and everyone else of coming judgment and exile. For the northern kingdom of Israel, God's time of mercy had expired. He extended mercy for hundreds of years, but now it was time for *no mercy*.

Then Gomer gave birth to a second son named **Lo-Ammi**. The name **Lo-Ammi** means "Not My People." Every call to this unfortunately named child reminded Hosea and everyone else that the people of Israel had pushed away the Lord God, and should no longer be considered His people.

Since Gomer did not give up her prostitution, there may have been a cruel irony in the name **Lo-Ammi**. Perhaps this son really was not the son of Hosea, but of another man. Perhaps the appearance of the child made this evident. You can almost picture Hosea and Gomer walking down the street pushing the baby carriage with little Lo-Ammi, who didn't look anything like either one of them. Someone asks about the name of the baby and Hosea answers, "Not My People." The message God had to deliver to Israel through Hosea was hard enough, but God also made Hosea *live* the message.

Summing up the meaning of the name Lo-Ammi, God said this to Israel through Hosea: **For you are not My people, and I will not be your God**: This was not so much of a *sentence* or a *penalty*, as it was a *simple stating of fact*. It wasn't as if the people of Israel really wanted to be the people of God, yet God would not have them. Instead, the people of Israel rejected God, and here the Lord simply recognized the fact. He would not play "let's pretend": "You pretend to be My people and I will pretend to be your God." The time for those games was over.

When we think about the relationship between Hosea and Gomer, there was a lot of pretending. Hosea pretended not to notice when she went out to prostitute herself. She came back pretending nothing ever happened. As much as they could, they pretended to be a happy family. God used the pretence in Hosea's family as an illustration of the pretence between Himself and His people. This brings it back to your relationship with God. Is it filled with pretence? Are you really a follower of Jesus Christ, or are you more of a pretender? What God did through Hosea shows us that God will allow that to continue for a time, but there comes a day when the pretence must end. Today should be that day.

TWO
Bible Reading: Hosea 2-3

CHOOSING A DIFFICULT KIND OF LOVE

Then the LORD said to me, "Go again, love a woman who is loved by a lover and is committing adultery, just like the love of the LORD for the children of Israel, who look to other gods and love the raisin cakes of the pagans." (Hosea 3:1)

God loves you. Perhaps you have heard or read those words a thousand or more times, and after a while they begin to lose their impact. They become just three words on a page and no longer amaze us. God knows all about this tendency in us; so He sends prophets to present the message in new and powerful ways.

God used the prophet Hosea to present the message of His love in an unforgettable way. God told him to marry a prostitute as a way to illustrate the amazing love God has for His people. Because of his cheating wife, Hosea had a unique perspective on how God *felt* about cheating Israel, who didn't faithfully love God the way that God loved them.

When God told Hosea, **Go again, love a woman who is loved by a lover and is committing adultery** He directed Hosea to go back to his wife, even though she was still **committing adultery**. It wasn't in the past; it was in the present. Yet the prophet was still commanded to go back to her and to **love** her. We learn two important principles from this.

First, Hosea stayed true to his marriage and did not divorce his wife even though she was clearly guilty of adultery. This shows us that though Deuteronomy 24:1 and Matthew 19:7-8 *permit* divorce when adultery breaks the marriage union, it by no means *commands* divorce. If God *commanded* divorce in the case of adultery, then God would have commanded Hosea to divorce his wife Gomer - but He didn't. Instead God told him, **Go again, love a woman who is loved by a lover and is committing adultery**.

Second, it shows us an important principle about love: Hosea was *directed to love, even when it must have been hard to love*. We are filled with many romantic illusions about love, and one of these illusions is that love has very little to do with our *will* - we are just "captured" by love and follow whatever course it leads. But in principle, the Scriptures show us another way: That love is largely a matter of the *will*, and when we direct ourselves to love someone God tells us we must love, it can and will happen. This is why "We're not in love anymore" isn't valid grounds for a bad relationship or divorce. It assumes that love is something beyond or outside of our will.

Your present feelings also don't justify a lack of love towards God. When the Bible says, "You shall love the LORD your God with all your heart, with all your soul, and with all your strength" (Deuteronomy 6:5) it directs the command towards our *will*. No matter what your feelings are, you can *choose* to love God today.

You can do it because the love God has for you is rooted in choice. That's why He told Hosea, **Just like the love of the LORD for the children of Israel**. This explains why God commanded Hosea to go back to his still-unfaithful wife. It was not only for the sake of Hosea and his wife Gomer, but also so that they would become a living lesson of the LORD's relationship with His people. Israel was still steeped in spiritual adultery, yet God still loved them.

For many, *choice* is the missing element in the way they love God and others. They wait to be swept away by feelings; instead, they are responsible to make the choice and then expect that the feelings will follow. If it seems like too much, think of the greatness of God's love and compassion towards you - that should make you much more loving, compassionate, and forgiving towards others. Make the right *choice* to love today.

THREE
Bible Reading: Hosea 4 and 5

THEY WILL NOT FIND HIM

With their flocks and herds they shall go to seek the LORD, but they will not find Him; He has withdrawn Himself from them.
(Hosea 5:6)

In the days of Hosea, ancient Israel knew what to do. They knew that they were expected to bring animal sacrifices to the LORD, both for atonement of sin and for fellowship with God. Yet it was possible to perform the action of sacrifice without a heart or life sacrificed to God - to make sacrifice an empty ritual. At the time Hosea the Prophet spoke to Israel, their worship was mainly empty rituals.

We see this in the words, **They shall go to seek the LORD, but they will not find Him**. Earlier, God promised through His prophet Hosea that He would leave rebellious Israel alone (Hosea 4:17). That meant that if they should make superficial gestures of repentance, **they will not find Him**. A few verses before this, God described their superficial repentance: *they do not direct their deeds toward turning to their God* (Hosea 5:4).

It's important to understand that there is a big difference between superficial religious gestures and a genuine turning of the heart towards God. In a moment of crisis someone may turn to God for relief - but have no real intention of surrendering their life to God.

In many ways today, people *think* they are seeking God when they really aren't. It's just a superficial investigation. For example, a man might say, "I grew up in the Baptist church and couldn't find God there. So I went to the Methodist church and couldn't find God there. Then I went to the Pentecostal church, but couldn't find God there. Now I'm at the Presbyterian church and can't find God." This man may imagine that he searched hard after God, but that is an illusion. The truth is that he is running away from God.

When God started to get close at the Baptist church, he left it and became a Methodist. When God started to get close to him at the Methodist church, he became a Pentecostal. This man followed the same pattern in each place - a superficial search for God that backed away when he really started getting close to God. Our sinful, fleshly nature doesn't mind religion and religious ritual - but it does whatever it can to keep us from really drawing close to God.

God does not reward this kind of superficial seeking. It might fool everyone else, but it doesn't fool God. Therefore Hosea announced the sad verdict: **He has withdrawn Himself from them**. It can happen. We can be so set in our sin and rebellion that God just leaves us to ourselves. Usually we don't even notice at first, but when we call upon the LORD and do **not find Him**, then we start to see the result of pushing God away.

Martin Luther was a very religious man before he personally experienced the truth of the Reformation, of being made right with God on the basis of *faith*. In his commentary on the Book of Galatians, Luther wrote eloquently about his religious devotion before coming to faith: "Outwardly I kept myself chaste, poor, and obedient. I was much given to fasting, watching, praying, saying of masses, and the like. Yet under the cloak of my outward respectability I continually mistrusted, doubted, feared, hated, and blasphemed God. My righteousness was a filthy puddle. Satan loves such saints."

Apart from a real relationship with God based on faith, religious traditions and works can't make us right with God. You may be frustrated because you seem to do so much for God, yet it seems that you do not **find Him**. Stop relying on empty rituals and come in faith. Let the promise of Jeremiah 29:14 be true for you: *I will be found by you, says the LORD.*

FOUR
Bible Reading: Hosea 6

WHAT GOD WANTS

*For I desire mercy and not sacrifice, and the knowledge
of God more than burnt offerings.* (Hosea 6:6)

In Hosea 5 God spoke against the empty religious rituals of His people. In chapter 6 of Hosea, the prophet told Israel what God wanted *instead* of empty sacrifices. He put it powerfully and eloquently: **For I desire mercy and not sacrifice, and the knowledge of God more than burnt offerings** (Hosea 6:6).

At this time the people of Israel were still good at bringing sacrifice but they had forsaken **mercy**, and they abandoned **mercy** because they gave up the knowledge of God and truth (Hosea 4:1). God wanted right hearts, full of truth and mercy, more than He wanted sacrifice. This wasn't to say that sacrifice was unimportant to God - it was a valued part of the covenant God made with Israel on Mount Sinai. Yet compared to **mercy** and **the knowledge of God**, sacrifice is far less important.

Hosea didn't just speak the heart of a distant God of the Old Testament - as a faithful prophet, he also revealed the same nature of God that was *perfectly* revealed in Jesus Christ. Jesus twice quoted this passage of Hosea to the religious leaders of His own day. He quoted this passage to them because they also missed the heart of God, focusing on the wrong and superficial things.

The first time Jesus quoted this passage is found in Matthew 9:13. He sat down to dinner with many notorious sinners, in an obvious attempt to reach out to these spiritually needy and hungry people. When the Pharisees criticized Him, Jesus answered: *"But go and learn what this means: 'I desire mercy and not sacrifice.'"* Jesus knew and remembered the message of Hosea and applied it to the situation at that moment.

The second time Jesus quoted Hosea 6:6 is found in Matthew 12:7. The context was again criticism by the Pharisees - but this time they criticized the disciples of Jesus instead of Jesus Himself. Jesus jumped to their defense and told the Pharisees: *"But if you had known what this means, 'I desire mercy and not sacrifice,' you would not have condemned the guiltless."* Jesus emphasized that God cares more about how we treat others than religious traditions or ceremonies.

In the Sermon on the Mount, Jesus seemed to speak with the heart of Hosea 6:6: *"Therefore if you bring your gift to the altar, and there remember that your brother has something against you, leave your gift there before the altar, and go your way. First be reconciled to your brother, and then come and offer your gift."* (Matthew 5:23-24) The idea is consistent. It's great for you to come to church and participate in worship and bring your gifts to God. Nevertheless, how you treat other people is more important. Get things right with others *before* you come before God. It's too easy for us to think, "I get along with God just fine. It's all those people I can't stand." If you aren't getting along with others, let the Holy Spirit do some serious soul-searching in you.

Hosea also told us that God values **the knowledge of God more than burnt offerings**. They missed what God really wants: a deep, close relationship with Him - expressed by the phrase, **the knowledge of God**.

Perhaps you do more for God than other people do. But are you *doing* something for God when He would rather you *first* get something right with another person? Are you *doing* something for God when He would rather you *first* draw closer to Him in **the knowledge of God**? Remember His priorities - and make them your priorities.

FIVE
Bible Reading: Hosea 7

LIKE A BAD PANCAKE

Ephraim has mixed himself among the peoples; Ephraim is a cake unturned. Aliens have devoured his strength, but he does not know it; yes, gray hairs are here and there on him, yet he does not know it. And the pride of Israel testifies to his face, but they do not return to the LORD their God, nor seek Him for all this. (Hosea 7:8-10)

God likes to talk in pictures. All through the Bible, the LORD uses word-pictures to tell us how He sees things. Hosea 7 is filled with word pictures describing the sinful character of ancient Israel in the days of the Prophet Hosea. In this chapter, God says Israel is like a thief or a band of robbers; like an adulterous wife; like a hot oven; and like a silly dove.

But my favorite word-picture from Hosea 7 is found in verses 8-10, where God called Israel **a cake unturned**. Don't let the address to **Ephraim** throw you off - Ephraim was the largest tribe of the 10 tribes that made up the northern kingdom, so sometimes God used the name "Ephraim" for the entire northern Kingdom of Israel.

The idea is of a "half-baked" cake. In that day, bread was often prepared as a cake that was cooked on both sides, something like a pancake. In thinking they could serve *both* the LORD and idols, Israel was like an **unturned** pancake - burned on one side, uncooked on the other.

This vividly describes the spiritual and moral condition of many people. They are *overexposed* to some things - perhaps the things of the world, the flesh, and the devil. Yet they are *underexposed* to other things - the things of God and His Spirit. Therefore, they are like **a cake unturned**. If you have ever made pancakes, you know what can be done with cakes that are burned on one side and uncooked on the other - *nothing*. You can't fix it by flipping it over, because the one side is still burned. The only thing you can do is scrape it off the griddle and toss it in the trash. In the same way, when someone is overexposed to the world and underexposed to God, God can't do much with that person.

Because of their spiritual decline, Israel was in danger: **Aliens have devoured his strength, but he does not know it**. This made the tragedy of Israel's ruin worse. The nation was being ravaged by sin but **does not know it**. They should know it, because even **the pride of Israel testifies to his face** - yet in their blind ignorance **they do not return to the LORD their God**.

To describe the self-deception of Israel, Hosea used another word-picture: **Yes, gray hairs are here and there on him, yet he does not know it**. In Hosea's day, Israel was as foolish as an old man who thought and acted like he was still young. We think it is a joke when an old, gray-headed man dresses in the most modern fashions and uses the slang of young people. We wonder, "Who does this old guy think he is fooling?" God thinks the same thing about us when we deceive ourselves about our spiritual condition.

- Burned and ruined - but he does not know it.
- Strength devoured - but he does not know it.
- Aging and weakening - but he does not know it.
- Pride testifies against him - but he does not know it.

It was said of Samson after Delilah cut his hair: "*But he did not know that the LORD had departed from him*" (Judges 16:20). This is where the people of Israel were, and where some followers of God are today. They are far from God and already suffering the effects, but they can't see it. Ask God to open your eyes today - not only to see Him, but also to see your *true* spiritual condition. Seeing both clearly make the path to true spiritual health.

SIX
Bible Reading: Hosea 8

A GREAT THING OR A STRANGE THING

*I have written for him the great things of My law, but
they were considered a strange thing* (Hosea 8:12)

Hosea spoke to the Kingdom of Israel - the ten northern tribes. They knew how to perform religious ceremonies, but they didn't really get right with God. In their sin and idolatry, Israel also rejected the Word of God. God had **great things** for Israel, but the **great things** seemed like a **strange thing** because their hearts were far from God.

This simple verse from Hosea tells us a lot about the Bible. First, it tells us the *author* of the Bible when it says, **I have written for him**. God Himself wrote the Bible. This is something many people *say* and many people *think*, but few people take to heart. If this book really is the message of the living God to a needy world, we need to take it far more seriously than most people do. We need to hear the words of the Prophet Hosea, and realize that the Bible was written by God.

Second, this verse tells us the *content* of the Bible - **great things**. Through Hosea, God spoke of **The great things of My law**. The Bible is filled with **great things**. It tells us about a great God, about a great Creator, His great love, man's great need, His great wisdom, His great sacrifice at great cost, our great redemption, and our great destiny. There is nothing in the Bible that is unimportant. Every verse connects to an important idea or principle. Remember the familiar words of 2 Timothy 3:16-17: *"All Scripture is given by inspiration of God, and is profitable for doctrine, for reproof, for correction, for instruction in righteousness, that the man of God may be complete, thoroughly equipped for every good work."* Because the Bible is filled with **great things** it has something to say to us.

Sometimes people think that the Bible isn't so great because they think "science" is superior. But as Charles Spurgeon said, "The science of Jesus Christ is the most excellent of sciences." No one should turn away from the Bible thinking that it isn't a book of science and learning. If the astronomer discovers distant galaxies, that is a very good thing - but it is a **great thing** to discover the Sun of Righteousness (Malachi 4:2) and the Star of Bethlehem. The botanist who studies the world of plants does a very good thing - but it is a **great thing** to study Jesus, who is called the Lily of the Valley and the Rose of Sharon. The geologist who researches rocks and mineralogy does a very good thing - but it is a **great thing** to read of the Rock of Ages and the White Stone each of the redeemed will receive. The history of the world is important and is a good thing to study and understand, but it is a **great thing** to know the history of the Bible, which records the record of God's dealing with man and man's dealing with God.

Third, this verse tells us *how the Bible is received by the natural man*: **But they were considered a strange thing**. The Bible might be **strange** because it is unknown or distant, or it might be **strange** because one doesn't like the message. Paul expressed the same idea in 1 Corinthians 2:14: *But the natural man does not receive the things of the Spirit of God, for they are foolishness to him; nor can he know them, because they are spiritually discerned.* The Word of God and the things of His Spirit are **great things**, but they seem like a **strange thing** when man is in sin and idolatry.

Here is a great one-minute spiritual check up: is the Bible a **great thing** or a **strange thing** to you? If it is a **great thing**, do you *live* as if the Bible were a **great thing**? Take it personally - the Bible is God's **great thing** for you.

SEVEN
Bible Reading: Hosea 9

A PAUSE TO GIVE PAUSE

Give them, O LORD; what will You give? Give them a miscarrying womb and dry breasts! (Hosea 9:14)

When He first brought Israel out of Egypt, God delighted in His people and they loved Him in return. It didn't stay that way. God loved Israel and treated them as something wonderful, and in response Israel cheated on God like an unfaithful spouse cheats on their marriage partner. It got so bad that "*They became an abomination like the thing they loved*" (Hosea 9:10). Israel loved their disgraceful idols, and they became like them. We do become like the god we love and serve, whether that means becoming like the LORD or becoming like an *abomination*.

As you might imagine, all of this was tremendously frustrating to Hosea. He saw Israel's sin and cried out against it. He saw them locked into the same sinful patterns for years. He saw Israel becoming like the disgusting idols they insisted on serving. Yet he knew that he was different - Hosea looked into his own heart and knew that *he* wasn't like that.

Out of that context comes the opening exclamation of Hosea 9:14: **Give them, O LORD - What will You give?** The idea is that Hosea began an angry prayer against the people (**Give them, O LORD**). In his angry prayer, Hosea would probably ask for judgment and ruin upon Israel. After all, they *deserved* it. Yet it seems that just as he began his angry prayer, the Spirit of God checked the heart of the prophet and he made an important pause, not knowing what to pray (**What will you give?**). This was a pause that should give us pause. The prophet prayed from a position of spiritual superiority. "LORD, I'm righteous and these wicked people of Israel are not. You better give it to them good, God!" In the pause between **Give them,**

O LORD and **What will You give?** Hosea realized that his own heart wasn't right and an angry prayer changed into a prayer of compassion.

In the end, he asked for **a miscarrying womb and dry breasts**. Really, Hosea prayed for *mercy*. Hosea looked ahead and he saw the terrible and certain judgment coming upon Israel. Because of their sin and rejection of God, it could be no other. Yet instead of rejoicing in that judgment (in a bitter, "give it to them LORD!" way), he was now horrified by the reality of that judgment. He knew it was coming but he couldn't rejoice in it. He had God's own heart when it came to the necessary but reluctant work of bringing judgment to His own people. Therefore, knowing the coming judgment, he prayed "LORD, give them few children so those children will not have to face the horrors of Your coming judgment." He didn't think that **a miscarrying womb and dry breasts** were a direct blessing to Israel, but in the environment of coming judgment they were an indirect blessing.

In this we find an enduring lesson. Sometimes those who see themselves - perhaps accurately - as more spiritual and closer to God than others in a church or group get angry and frustrated with others who don't seem to have hearts burning for the LORD. Their frustration is understandable but the pause in Hosea's prayer should give them pause. The prayer that started in anger and bitterness was paused and transformed into a pained prayer for a glimmer of indirect blessing, even in the midst of judgment.

Do you long for revival and spiritual passion among God's people? Do you sense that you have something in your walk with God that other Christians should have? Please know that if these factors make you proud, angry, or bitter against others then Satan has won a great victory. Keep praying for a great work of God among His people in general, but don't forget that He has more of a work to do in you - and let the prophet's pause in the midst of an angry prayer give you pause, guarding you from the cancer of spiritual pride.

EIGHT

Bible Reading: Hosea 10

ADVICE TO EVERY FARMER

Sow for yourselves righteousness; reap in mercy; break up your fallow ground, for it is time to seek the LORD, till He comes and rains righteousness on you. (Hosea 10:12)

The way the Prophet Hosea saw the situation, everyone in Israel was a farmer - even if they made their money in some other way. Hosea, speaking as the mouthpiece of the LORD, thought everyone was a farmer in the sense that we all *sow* things with our life and *reap* a result from what we have sown.

Sadly, as the previous chapters of the Book of Hosea show, Israel had sown very bad seed. They had a harvest of judgment to reap from the bad seed - yet even then, Hosea made a promise: **Sow for yourselves righteousness; reap in mercy**. Even then, if they would sow **righteousness**, they would **reap in mercy** at the next harvest.

If the Prophet Hosea were among us today, he would tell each of us that we are also farmers. We all sow into our life but do we **sow** seeds of **righteousness**? What will come of the seeds you planted today, or this past week, or this past month? This should give each of us thoughtful pause. A thought becomes an action, and an action becomes a pattern. A pattern becomes a habit, and a habit becomes a life. Our actions do not stand all by themselves; they are also steps on a road, and it is worth considering where that road ends.

Hosea tells us how to make a better road: **Break up your fallow ground**. God built on the picture of sowing and reaping by telling Israel to **break up your fallow ground** - ground that hasn't been plowed for more than a year. It is ground that is hard and stubborn, resistant to the seed. It does little good to sow seed on **fallow ground**; it must be broken up first. Several times in the Bible, God's word is likened to a seed that is planted in the human heart. Sometimes when the word of God goes forth and seems to have little effect, it is because it falls on **fallow ground** - hard earth. Something must change in this hard ground that will not allow the seed of the word to penetrate and become fruitful.

Since **fallow ground** is hard, it probably doesn't want to be broken up. It is hard and compact, and the blade of the plow hurts as it cuts through. If the **fallow ground** could talk, it would probably cry out when it is plowed. Yet it is useless as a place for seed as long as it is **fallow**.

Hosea also told us *how* to break up the fallow ground: **For it is time to seek the LORD.** We break up the fallow ground by seeking the LORD, not our self or idols.

Hosea told us *when* to break up the fallow ground: **For it is time** shows that the time to break up the fallow ground is *now*. Don't wait; the ground just gets harder each day.

Hosea told us *how long* to work on breaking up the fallow ground: **Till He comes and rains righteousness on you**. Though it is difficult work, and though the ground resists the effort of the plow to break it up, we stay with this work. We stay with it *until blessing from God is evident*. The rain from heaven will not only water and nourish the hard ground, it will also *help the work of softening the hard ground*. This shows that when the believer works to soften the hard ground of his heart, the Spirit of God is close by to bless that work. We must do it until God's blessing is evident again.

God's use of the figures of sowing and reaping remind us that our harvest is sometimes a season away. Sometimes people expect to sow sin for years, but to immediately **reap in mercy** after sowing **righteousness** for one day. Stick with sowing in righteousness, you will **reap in mercy** in due time.

NINE
Bible Reading: Hosea 11

WITH GENTLE CORDS

I taught Ephraim to walk, taking them by their arms; but they did not know that I healed them. I drew them with gentle cords, with bands of love, and I was to them as those who take the yoke from their neck. I stooped and fed them. (Hosea 11:3-4)

The tribe of Ephraim was the dominant tribe of the Northern Kingdom of Israel, so often in the Book of Hosea God spoke to Israel through the name "Ephraim." In this passage, God reminded Israel through Hosea of His tender love: **I taught Ephraim to walk...but they did not know that I healed them**. God did a lot for Israel that they were never aware of. The same principle is true in our relationship with God - we often are blessed and protected by God far beyond what we can see.

He guided them along the way, **taking them by their arms**. The picture is of a parent teaching a child how to walk by holding the child's arms and supporting the child as they make their awkward steps. It is easy to see in your mind's eye: a toddler's halting steps, with the loving father holding each upraised hand of the child, guiding it along the way with strength and balance. The father knows that if he were to let go the child would fall, so **taking them by their arms** he holds on. It's a tender picture of our tender God.

Knowing Israel had to return to the LORD, God set about doing it in His powerful, gentle way: **I drew them with gentle cords, with bands of love**. Even when God draws His people, it is with **gentle cords** of **love**, not with harsh manipulation or coercion. God wants to win us over, but not with brute force. He has the power and perhaps even the right to simply overpower our will and *make us* choose Him. But He doesn't work that way. His will is to woo, and He definitely draws us - yet He draws us **with gentle cords, with bands of love**.

God does it this way because He wants more than our obedience - He wants our *love*. He knows that once our love is freely given to Him, then obedience will follow. God doesn't want slaves or robots in His servants, but free men and women who freely choose Him - drawn **with gentle cords, with bands of love**.

In the ancient world, the empires of Persia and Greece fought bitter wars. There was said to be a great difference between their soldiers. In the Persian army, soldiers were like slaves and driven into battle with whips and threats. In the Greek army, soldiers were free men and patriots, and fought for Sparta and Greece out of love for country and a sense of duty. The smaller armies of Greece usually beat the larger armies of Persia. God calls us as an army of free men, grateful patriots of the kingdom of God.

When we accept the drawing action of God, the reward is great. God said through Hosea that He was to Israel, **as those who take the yoke from their neck**. This refers to relaxing and loosening the yoke-collar of a plowing animal, giving the animal rest and the freedom to breathe. Drawn by gentle cords to Him, we then find our burden easy and His yoke light.

How much does God want this for you? The prophet Hosea gives you a clue when he said on God's behalf to Israel, **I stooped and fed them**. God humbled Himself to minister to His needy people. One might almost think it is beneath the dignity and honor of God to stoop so low for His people, but He never thinks so. Jesus stooped all the way from the ivory palaces of heaven to the humiliating death of the cross (Philippians 2) and He did it all to draw you **with gentle cords, with bands of love**. Have you thanked Him for it lately?

TEN
Bible Reading: Hosea 11

GOD, AND NOT MAN

I will not execute the fierceness of My anger; I will not again destroy Ephraim. For I am God, and not man, the Holy One in your midst; and I will not come with terror. (Hosea 11:9)

Hosea saw the dark clouds of judgment on the horizon for Israel. Even so, God took no pleasure in the chastening about to come upon His people. Instead He said, *"My sympathy is stirred"* (Hosea 11:8). In that same verse He looked at the tragedy about to come upon Israel, and even though they deserved it He still asked, *"How can I give you up, Ephraim?"*

Without God, man is in the same place. We are in sin, and are guilty before God. Yet He says, **How can I give you up?** Justice demands that He do this, yet in His heart He must find a way of salvation. In this, God sent Jesus Christ and on the cross Jesus was "given up" in our place.

In Hosea 11:8, it was as if God was distraught over the destruction to come. God says, "I can't bear to allow My people to be caught up in the destruction that will come upon all the nations, as *Admah* and *Zeboiim* (mentioned in Hosea 11:8) were caught up in the destruction that came upon Sodom and Gomorrah." Deuteronomy 29:23 tells us the sad fate of these two cities.

In the midst of this God made a solemn promise: **I will not again destroy Ephraim**. Though their sin deserved it, God would not wipe out Israel. He would leave a remnant, and would restore the nation. This promise of restoration proved something God said about Himself: when it comes to forgiveness and restoration, **I am God, and not man**.

The longsuffering, forgiveness, and compassion of the LORD toward His people seems unbelievable until we recognize that He is

not man, but God. His love and forgiveness are of a different kind. There are many differences between God and man in the matter of forgiveness.

- Man cannot hold back his anger very long - but God does.
- Man will not reconcile if the person who offended him is a person of bad character - but Jesus Christ died for the ungodly.
- Man is often only willing to be reconciled if the offending party craves forgiveness and makes the first move - but God makes the first move toward us.
- Man is often only willing to be reconciled if the offending party will promise to never again do the wrong - but God reconciles knowing we may sin in the same area again.
- Man, when he does reconcile, does not lift the former offender to place of high status and partnership - but God adopts us and makes us His co-workers.
- Man, when he is wronged, does not bear all of the penalty for the wrong done - but on the cross, Jesus Christ bore all the guilt our sin deserved.
- Man, when he attempts reconciliation, will not continue if he is rejected - but God keeps offering forgiveness even when we first reject it.
- Man will not restore an offender without a period of probation - God requires no probationary period.
- Man will not love, adopt, honor, and associate with one who has wronged him - God adopts us as His sons and daughters.
- Man will not trust someone who has formerly wronged them - God lifts us up to heavenly places to reign with Him.

What often passes for forgiveness among men is nothing like the amazing forgiveness of God. We should be thankful for this, and make our forgiveness to others more like the amazing forgiveness God has given us.

ELEVEN
Bible Reading: Hosea 12

HOW TO FIGHT GOD AND WIN

He took his brother by the heel in the womb, and in his strength he struggled with God. Yes, he struggled with the Angel and prevailed; he wept, and sought favor from Him. He found Him in Bethel, and there He spoke to us. (Hosea 12:3-4)

Through the Prophet Hosea, God spoke to Israel using an ancient name - Jacob. Of course, the name "Israel" was first given to Jacob, the grandson of Abraham. God looked at Israel in Hosea's day and put before them the example of their ancient ancestor.

Jacob was famous because at his birth, "**he took his brother by the heel in the womb**." He literally came out of the womb with his hand on his brother's heel (Genesis 25:26). As God looked back at the patriarch Jacob, He saw that Israel in Hosea's day was just like their forefather Jacob in the days of Genesis. In ancient Israel, a "heel-catcher" was a double-dealer, someone who achieved their goals through crafty and dishonest ways. Through Hosea, God said, "That was Jacob then and it is Israel now."

Then, the prophet did a fast-forward and looked at another event in the life of Jacob, when "**in his strength he struggled with God**." The prophet recalled the struggle between Jacob and the Man of Genesis 32:24-30. Jacob refused to submit to God, so God demanded submission from him in a literal wrestling match. Jacob had one of the most fantastic athletic contests of all time - a wrestling match with God. We may speak spiritually of wrestling with God in prayer, or wrestling in spiritual warfare, but Jacob's wrestling was physical as well as spiritual. He was locked in competition with God in human form.

Hosea's words "**he struggled with God**" reinforced a point already made clear in Genesis 32:24-30: Jacob wrestled with the

Lord God, who appeared in human form as a Man. Since this was a unique messenger from heaven, He was also described as an **Angel** of the Lord.

Inspired by the Holy Spirit, Hosea emphasized two more details from the Genesis account: "**He struggled with the Angel and prevailed; he wept, and sought favor from Him**." First, he tells us that Jacob **prevailed** in the wrestling match. Second, he tells us that Jacob **wept** in the struggle. He **prevailed** in the only way anyone can when they struggle against God. We prevail when we lose and know it, surrendering to God.

It is also important to know that Jacob **wept**, because it helps us understand how desperate and broken he was as he hung on the Lord, and only plead for a blessing. On a physical level, Jacob lost. God touched his hip and took him out of the competition. Having wrestled all night, Jacob limped back to his family that morning a loser. But Jacob won spiritually; he clung to God until blessing was promised.

In what ways do you wrestle with God? There are many opportunities to resist what God wants to do. You may not physically strain against Him as Jacob did, but your resistance may be just as real. Your hope of successfully resisting God is destined to be disappointed.

Losing when you struggle against God is a good thing. It brings you back to something we all need to remember: that God is the Creator, and I am His creature. There is a comfort in knowing and walking in our "creatureliness." I can look up to God and honor Him as the One who genuinely deserves to be my Lord. He has won me over.

Today, you can win when you fight God - win by letting Him win you over. Make your prayer something like this: "Lord, help me to see ways that I am resisting you today. In those areas, please win me over. And when I find you winning me over, let me look for Your blessing in my losing."

TWELVE
Bible Reading: Hosea 13

TAKE WORDS WITH YOU

O Israel, return to the LORD your God, for you have stumbled because of your iniquity; take words with you, and return to the LORD. Say to Him, "Take away all iniquity; receive us graciously, for we will offer the sacrifices of our lips. Assyria shall not save us, we will not ride on horses, nor will we say anymore to the work of our hands, 'You are our gods.' for in You the fatherless finds mercy." (Hosea 14:1-3)

Hosea is a tough book - not that it is so tough to understand, but when you do understand it you see that it is full of God's strong warnings of judgment against His wayward people. Yet this last chapter of Hosea is beautiful and packed with precious promises. It shows that where sin abounds, grace abounds even more. We thought maybe the book would end with a crescendo of judgment, but it overflows with grace.

In the opening of the chapter, Hosea told Israel *how* to return to God: "**Take words with you, and return to the LORD.**" God told them to come like this: "When you return to Me, **take words with you**. I want you to return to Me not with a silent feeling in your heart, but with proper words of repentance and trust in Me."

When you come before the LORD, it is essential to **take words with you**. There is a place for sharing the inarticulate feelings of the heart with God, but that is not the essence of fellowship and prayer with Him. True worship is intelligent and God made us able to communicate ideas and feelings with words. It isn't enough to sit before the LORD and feel love towards Him. Instead, **take words with you** - *tell God that you love Him*. It isn't enough to feel repentance before the LORD. **Take words with you** and *tell God you repent before Him*.

This is the same idea that Paul expressed in Romans 10:9-10: "*That if you confess with your mouth the Lord Jesus and believe in your heart that God has raised Him from the dead, you will be saved. For with the heart one believes unto righteousness, and with the mouth confession is made unto salvation.*" God commands us to communicate with Him in **words**, not only in ideas or feelings. What words do we take with us? Take the words God gives you in His Word! When we communicate to God in the words and ideas of Scripture, we find an articulate and effective voice before God.

Come to God asking for forgiveness and mercy: "**Take away all iniquity; receive us graciously**." When we return to the LORD, taking words with us, we must first come humbly. We recognize our sin and our total dependence on the grace of God.

Literally, Hosea 14:2 says *for we will offer the calves of our lips.* Since bull calves were often brought for sacrifice, the translators felt justified in putting it "**for we will offer the sacrifices of our lips.**" However, the more literal rendering shows just how plainly our words of praise, worship, confession, petition, or intercession can be a sacrifice before God.

The idea carries on: "**Assyria shall not save us, we will not ride on horses, nor will we say anymore to the work of our hands, 'You are our gods'.**" When we return to the LORD, taking words with us, we come renouncing our dependence on all other things. We recognize that the LORD and the LORD alone can make the difference in our life.

Finally, return to the LORD recognizing His goodness: "**For in You the fatherless finds mercy.**" When we return to the LORD, taking words with us, we come declaring His greatness. We tell of what a great and merciful God we have.

So come to God, and take words with you. Come asking for forgiveness and mercy. Come offering a sacrifice of praise. Come renouncing dependence on anything else. And come recognizing His goodness. Just come.

THIRTEEN
Bible Reading: Hosea 14

BLESSINGS TO HEALED BACKSLIDERS

I will heal their backsliding, I will love them freely, for My anger has turned away from him. I will be like the dew to Israel; he shall grow like the lily, and lengthen his roots like Lebanon. His branches shall spread; his beauty shall be like an olive tree, and his fragrance like Lebanon. Those who dwell under his shadow shall return; they shall be revived like grain, and grow like a vine. Their scent shall be like the wine of Lebanon. (Hosea 14:4-7)

Throughout the Book of Hosea, God spoke to a backslidden Israel. Here God made a great promise: "**I will heal their backsliding**." God saw that Israel was bent on backsliding from Him (Hosea 11:7), but He promised to heal a *repentant* Israel. He did not do it because Israel deserved it, as if their repentance earned this special touch from God. Instead, God did it because it is in His nature to **love them freely**. On the basis of that great love, He made a great promise: "**I will heal their backsliding**."

This promise is *compassionate*. "**I will heal their backsliding**" shows that God looks on our **backsliding** more like a *disease* than a *crime*. He did not say, "I will pardon their backsliding." It is as if God sees His poor, weak people and remembers that they are only dust. He remembers that they easily fall prey to a hundred temptations through the fall and they quickly go astray. Yet in His kindness, God treats them not as rebels but as patients, and He wants His people to look on Him as a physician.

The promise is *certain*. "**I will heal their backsliding**" is a definite word. God did not say, "I might heal" or "I could heal" or "I can try to heal," but I *will* **heal their backsliding**. This assures us that if we come to God for healing of our backsliding, He **will** do it! God is too great a physician to allow any patient to leave without being healed.

The word is *personal.* "**I will heal their backsliding**" speaks of specific people; God addressed them personally. We have to come to the Great Physician and say, "Heal *my* backsliding. I want to be one of the '**their**.'" Yet to get the healing, you have to count yourself among the backsliders.

The word is *powerful.* When God says, "**I will heal their backsliding**" He doesn't mean a little or a partial healing. His intention is to do a complete restoration. This passage shows us how much is restored when we return to the LORD from a season of backsliding.

- *Growth* is restored (**He shall grow**).
- *Beauty* is restored (**He shall grow like the lily**).
- *Strength* is restored (**lengthen his roots like Lebanon**).
- *Value* is restored (**His beauty shall be like an olive tree**).
- *Delight* is restored (**His fragrance like Lebanon**).
- *Abundance* is restored (**revived like grain...grow like the vine...scent shall be like the wine of Lebanon**).

Best of all, the promise of restoration means that the formerly backslidden one will become *a blessing* to others. "**His branches will spread**" suggests a broad tree that provides fruit, shade, and shelter to others. When God restores His people they then become a blessing to others, not only blessed themselves.

Are you backsliding? The signs may not be so obvious to other people who see your life. When you see a tree broken over in a windstorm, it's easy to think that it was the power of the wind that made the tree topple. But often, if you look closer, you may see that insects were at work a long time on the tree, making it weaker and weaker. It really wasn't the wind that did it - other trees around it withstood the wind. It was the slow decline of strength, as insects nibbled away month after month. Don't let the cancer of a backslidden relationship with God nibble away at your strength. Take Him up on His gracious and generous promise of restoration.

FOURTEEN
Bible Reading: Joel 1

HOW TO GET RIGHT

Gird yourselves and lament, you priests; wail, you who minister before the altar; come, lie all night in sackcloth, you who minister to my God; for the grain offering and the drink offering are withheld from the house of your God. Consecrate a fast, call a sacred assembly; gather the elders and all the inhabitants of the land into the house of the LORD your God, and cry out to the LORD. (Joel 1:13-14)

Most of the prophets warned that judgment was coming, and they invited God's people to be spared by turning to the LORD. The Book of Joel is different - he simply observed that judgment was *here* and told them what to do about it. It's hard to pin down his exact time, because he doesn't mention any other kings or prophets. Many scholars date the book of Joel to 835 B.C.

It was a time of turmoil and transition in Judah, at the end of the reign of the Queen Mother Athaliah and the beginning of the reign of King Joash. Athaliah seized power at the sudden death in battle of her son Ahaziah, who only reigned one year (2 Kings 8:26, 2 Kings 11:1). Athaliah killed all her son's heirs, except for one who was hidden in the temple and escaped - one-year-old Joash (2 Kings 11:3).

During her six years as queen over Judah, Athaliah reigned wickedly. She was the granddaughter of the wicked King Omri of Israel - making her daughter or niece to Ahab, one of Israel's worst kings (2 Kings 8:26). If we are accurate in thinking that Joel prophesied in 835 B.C. then the judgment he described came toward the end of the six-year reign of ungodliness under Queen Athaliah. No wonder God brought a heavy hand on Judah! Now, notice what Joel told the people of God to do.

First, they were told to "**gird yourselves and lament, you priests**." Joel called the religious leaders to lead the nation in repentance. He told the priests to **gird yourselves** for repentance, and the idea was that they should "prepare to do the work of repentance."

Joel went on to tell them *how* to do the work of repentance.

- "**Consecrate a fast**": Make getting right with God so important that even eating isn't important.
- "**Call a sacred assembly**": Call for God's people to come together and repent.
- "**Gather the elders**": The leaders of the people should make a special point to be part of the work of repentance.
- "**Into the house of the LORD your God**": Come to the place where you *should* meet together with God.
- "**And cry out unto the LORD**": Finally, simply cry out to God and trust that He will respond in mercy.

In this time of drought, all Judah could do was **cry out** to God. They were powerless to "fix" the drought problem. God sent them to a place where only heaven could help them, so that they would look no other place.

In Luke 13:1-5 Jesus was confronted with the problem of a disaster that killed 18 people. Instead of acting as if it were just an accident of blind fate, Jesus used it as a wake-up call for repentance. Jesus showed that "Why did this disaster happen to them?" is the wrong question to ask. The right question is "Am I ready to face such a disaster in this fallen world?"

Are you ready?

FIFTEEN
Bible Reading: Joel 2

WHAT TO TEAR

*"Now, therefore," says the LORD, "Turn to Me with all your heart,
with fasting, with weeping, and with mourning." So rend your
heart, and not your garments; return to the LORD your God, for He is
gracious and merciful, slow to anger, and of great kindness; and He
relents from doing harm.* (Joel 2:12-13)

A good doctor knows how to apply the remedy to the place
where it is needed. If your feet hurt, only a bad doctor would give
you something to clear your sinuses. The same principle works in
spiritual things. When there is a spiritual problem, God speaks right
to the afflicted area – and keeps speaking to it until the area is healed.

In that context, God told Judah, through His prophet, that they
must "**Turn to Me with all your heart, with fasting, with weeping,
and with mourning**." Earlier Joel warned Judah that though they
were in a tough time, worse judgment would come unless they got
right with God. Now he told them to respond - *because* they heard
the warning of judgment, God's people should repent and to do it
sincerely:

• Sincere repentance is to "**turn to**" God, and therefore *away
from* our sin.
• Sincere repentance is done "**with all your heart**," giving
everything you can in surrender to God.
• Sincere repentance is marked by *action* (**with fasting**)
and *emotion* (**with weeping...mourning**). Not every act of
repentance will include **fasting** and **weeping**, but if *action*
and *emotion* are absent, it isn't sincere repentance.

Phony repentance offends God. This is what he spoke against
with the words, "**Rend your heart, and not your garments**." One
expression of mourning in Jewish culture is tearing the clothes. It

was a way to say, "I am so overcome with grief that don't care if my clothes are ruined and I look bad." Joel knew that one could tear their **garments** without tearing their **heart**, and he described the kind of heart-repentance that really pleased God. A ripped heart is a more certain sign of real repentance than a ripped shirt.

In one of his great sermons, Charles Spurgeon told the story of a woman who came seeming to be in great sorrow, saying what a great sinner she was. Yet Spurgeon suspected her repentance wasn't sincere. He said to her, "Well, if you are a sinner of course you have broken God's laws. Let's read the Ten Commandments and see which ones you have broken." They started at the first: "You shall have no other gods before Me," and Spurgeon asked her if she ever broke that commandment. "Oh no," she said, "not that I know of." As you might suppose, Spurgeon went through all Ten Commandments and the supposedly repentant woman could not find a single one that she had broken, and what he suspected about her was true. She didn't really consider herself a sinner, and she was making a show of repentance because she thought it was expected of her. This woman needed to hear God's message through Joel: "**Rend your heart, and not your garments**."

If real repentance is such a deep work, it's easy to think that it isn't really worth it. Joel reminds us all that it *is* worth it: "**Return to the LORD your God, for He *is* gracious and merciful, slow to anger, and of great kindness; and He relents from doing harm**." This was another encouragement to repentance. The first was present chastisement, and the second was the threat of coming judgment; but knowing the goodness and mercy of God is another motive for true repentance. We come to Him confident that He will heal and forgive, and that He may relent from the judgment He announced.

Take God's goodness as motivation to *real* repentance – a repentance of the heart, not only of external things. Tear your heart, and not your clothes.

SIXTEEN
Bible Reading: Joel 2

SOMETHING SPECIAL FOR EVERYONE

And it shall come to pass afterward that I will pour out My Spirit on all flesh; your sons and your daughters shall prophesy, your old men shall dream dreams, your young men shall see visions. And also on My menservants and on My maidservants I will pour out My Spirit in those days." (Joel 2:28-29)

The Book of Joel begins with fearful warnings of judgment, but continues into glorious promises of restoration. Joel described a restoration closer to his own day, and also an ultimate restoration: **"It shall come to pass afterward."** This speaks of a greater time, of ultimate restoration and blessing. This latter time will be marked by an outpouring of God's **Spirit on all flesh** - not only selected men at selected times for selected duties.

The Old Testament has a rich record of the work of the Spirit, but He was not poured out **"on all flesh"** then. Instead, certain men were filled with the Spirit at certain times and only for certain duties. Here, Joel looked forward to something greater than all the previous individual and exceptional examples. He saw the glorious New Covenant, when the Spirit of God would be poured out **on all flesh**. Why, even *your* **sons and daughters**, *your* **old men**, and *your* **young men** would be filled with the Spirit of God.

This was fulfilled on the Day of Pentecost when the disciples gathered in the upper room, waiting in Jerusalem for the outpouring of the Holy Spirit that Jesus promised would come (Acts 1:4-5). When the outpouring of the Spirit came, the 120 followers of Jesus were all filled with the Spirit and began to praise God in other tongues. Jerusalem was crowded at that time, because of the feast of Pentecost - so a crowd quickly gathered because of the commotion. Those who heard the disciples praise God in these miraculous languages began to mock them, claiming they were drunk. Peter stood up and boldly set the record straight: the disciples were not drunk at all, but this was a fulfillment of Joel's great prophecy of the outpouring of the Spirit.

At first, any Jew of that day might scoff at the idea of 120 followers of a crucified man being filled with the Holy Spirit. Based on their understanding of the Old Testament they would think, "These 120 people are not kings, prophets, priests; God only pours out His Spirit on special people for special duties. These are common folk, and God doesn't pour out His Spirit on them." Peter used the prophecy of Joel to show that things were different then, just as God said they would be. Now, the Holy Spirit was poured out upon all who believed and received, even the common folk. Now God offered a New Covenant relationship, and part of the New Covenant was the outpouring of the Spirit for all who receive in faith.

The idea is repeated several times for emphasis: "**And also on My menservants and on My maidservants**." In this latter time, all the servants of the LORD will be filled with His Spirit in this unique and powerful way. Under the New Covenant, every believer can receive the full measure of the Spirit and be used in a special and wonderful way.

Sometimes the common churchgoer simply wants a building to worship in, a nice service that isn't too offensive, and a good sermon - after that he thinks, *leave me alone*. That isn't New Covenant Christianity, which sees the work of the ministry as belonging to the people, not to the "clergy." The clear teaching of Scripture says that the work of the ministry belongs to all the people of God, and it is the job of God-appointed offices and ministries to equip the people of God for this (Ephesians 4:7-16).

Joel saw it hundreds of years before the fulfillment – God has a unique empowering of His Spirit for all who belong to the New Covenant. Today, *believe* Him for it, *receive* it from Him, *walk* in the empowering He supplies, and *thank* Him for such a generous outpouring.

SEVENTEEN
Bible Reading: Joel 2

CALLING WHOEVER

And it shall come to pass that whoever calls on the name of the LORD shall be saved. For in Mount Zion and in Jerusalem there shall be deliverance, as the LORD has said, among the remnant whom the LORD calls. (Joel 2:32)

It's an amazing statement: "**Whoever calls on the name of the LORD shall be saved**." This glorious promise associated with the time Joel said "**Shall come to pass**" afterward. In this time of the poured-out Spirit of God, salvation will no longer be a matter of association with national Israel. Instead, "**Whoever calls on the name of the LORD shall be saved**" - no matter what nation they come from.

This is a broad call – "*Whoever* **calls on the name of the LORD shall be saved**." You might even say that this "whoever" is better than having your own name written in the Bible. If I read, "David Guzik shall be saved," my first reaction would be elation. I would *know* that God promised David Guzik would be saved. Then I would begin to think: "I'm not the only David Guzik in the world. I've done a Google search and have found a few others. And who is to say how many David Guziks there have been through history? Maybe I'm not the *right* David Guzik who will be saved." But when the Scriptures say, "*Whoever* **calls on the name of the LORD shall be saved**" then you *know* you are included in that. It's better than having your own name written in the Bible!

This is a call to prayer – "**Whoever *calls* on the name of the LORD shall be saved**." True prayer is calling on the name of the LORD, and you can't perish if you are genuinely calling on the name of the LORD. Charles Spurgeon wrote, "You cannot perish praying; no one has ever done so. If you could perish praying, you would be a new wonder in the universe. A praying soul in hell is an utter impossibility."

This is a call to come to the true God – "**Whoever calls on the name of the *Lord* shall be saved**." Coming to a false god, a god of your own imagination will do you no good. The god of your mere *opinion* does not exist and cannot save you. You must come to the God of the Bible. Sadly, most people today worship a god of their own making. They don't make an image of clay or gold, but they build a god in their mind according to their own thoughts. They think what they want God to be, and they create Him in *their* image. But there is no salvation in a self-made deity. Don't trust in a god you have made yourself – trust only in the God of the Bible. Call on the **name of the Lord** and be saved.

This is a call to come to God intelligently – "**Whoever calls on *the name* of the Lord shall be saved**." In the ancient world, the **name** stood for the person and character of the one named. To call on the name of the Lord means that you know something of His person and character. You know His power, so you call upon His power. You know His mercy, so you call upon His mercy. You know His wisdom, so you call upon Him to help you in every difficulty.

This is a certain promise – "**Whoever calls on the name of the Lord *shall be saved*.**" It is a profound mystery why all do not accept this great invitation, but the text itself tells us that only a remnant receives it (**among the remnant whom the Lord calls**). Yet all who *do* come are certainly saved. God's very honor depends upon it.

We have the great invitation – to call upon the name of the Lord. It is up to us to accept it and to communicate the offer to others. "**Whoever calls on the name of the Lord shall be saved**."

EIGHTEEN
Bible Reading: Joel 3

THE LOGIC OF JUDGMENT

Indeed, what have you to do with Me, O Tyre and Sidon, and all the coasts of Philistia? Will you retaliate against Me? But if you retaliate against Me, swiftly and speedily I will return your retaliation upon your own head. (Joel 3:4)

The final chapter of the brief Book of Joel begins with severe warnings of judgment and ends with a beautiful promise of restoration. Speaking to the nations, God asked "**Will you retaliate against Me?**" God virtually challenged the nations to come against Him or His people. He vowed to **return your retaliation upon your own head** to those who came against Him or His people. He promises to give back in judgment just what the nations gave to God and to His people. It's very logical – in judgment, you get back what you deserve. It is just "**retaliation upon your own head**."

Judgment is about the only aspect of God's plan of the ages that is plainly logical. The grace and mercy of God are not plainly logical. Salvation by grace through faith is not plainly logical. The high standing and destiny of the believer in Jesus is not plainly logical. Judgment - God simply giving those who reject Him what they deserve - *is plainly logical*. It is as if God says to the wicked, "You rejected the saving logic of heaven, so I will give you the plain logic of earth: you will receive what you deserve before the holy court of My justice."

Therefore, through the Prophet Joel God warned the nations that mistreated His ancient people, "**I will sell your sons and your daughters into the hand of the people of Judah**." The nations treated God's people with contempt, and had no sense of their worth. Therefore, God would repay them with the contempt they put upon His people, vowing to "**return your retaliation upon your own head**."

As we look at the world today and through history, we see that it is always a losing proposition to persecute the people of God. Though we are rightly distressed at religious persecution today, we can take comfort in the fact that the persecutors always lose. We can see this in the fate of ten Roman Emperors who persecuted Christians:

- Emperor Nero lost 30,000 of his subjects to pestilence, had his armies utterly defeated in Britain, suffered a revolution in Armenia, and was so hated by the senators of Rome that they forced him to kill himself.
- Emperor Domitian was butchered by his own soldiers.
- Emperor Trajan died of a foul disease.
- Emperor Severus died miserably on a military campaign in Britain.
- Emperor Maximus was cut in pieces, together with his son.
- Emperor Decius died as an exile in a far country.
- Emperor Valerian was whipped to death by the King of Persia who captured him.
- Emperor Aurelian was killed by his own soldiers.
- Emperor Dioclesian poisoned himself.
- Emperor Maximum hanged himself.

You can't step on the smallest toe of the mystical body of Christ without the head, Jesus Christ Himself, asking "Why have you hurt Me?" All in all, it shows the logic of judgment. Since Jesus is one with His people, if one strikes out against His people, that one has struck out against Jesus. Paul found this out on the road to Damascus, when Jesus asked him, "*Saul, Saul, why are you persecuting Me?*" (Acts 9:4)

It's better to choose the illogic of God's grace, forgiveness, and mercy. We like the strange logic of grace and mercy over the strict logic of judgment. Thank Him for it today.

NINETEEN
Bible Reading: Amos 1

AMOS THE FARMER

The words of Amos, who was among the sheepbreeders of Tekoa, which he saw concerning Israel in the days of Uzziah king of Judah, and in the days of Jeroboam the son of Joash, king of Israel, two years before the earthquake. (Amos 1:1)

We have a tendency to think that God uses the brightest and the best. He must choose the most holy and talented to deliver His message or to advance His kingdom. The writings of the prophet Amos show us that this isn't true. The name **Amos** means *burden* or *burden bearer*. Since most of the prophecies of Amos concern coming judgment on either the nations surrounding Israel or judgment on Israel itself, he was a man with a *burden*.

The man God chose to carry this burden "**Was among the sheepbreeders of Tekoa.**" It seems that Amos had no formal theological or prophetic training, though there was a "school of the prophets," whose members were known as the *sons of the prophets* at that time (for example, see 1 Kings 20:35 or 2 Kings 2:3-15). Amos was a simple man, a farmer, who had been uniquely called to ministry. He was not a professional clergyman, but just "**Among the sheepbreeders of Tekoa.**"

Amos spoke of his background and calling in Amos 7:14-15: "*I was no prophet, nor was I a son of a prophet, but I was a sheepbreeder and a tender of sycamore fruit. Then the LORD took me as I followed the flock, and the LORD said to me, 'Go, prophesy to My people Israel.'*"

Amos used an unusual word to describe his occupation. Instead of calling himself a "shepherd," the literal ancient Hebrew calls Amos a "sheep raiser." Amos probably chose this title to emphasize the fact that he really was a shepherd, and not a "shepherd" in a symbolic, spiritual sense. The way God used Amos reminds us of the way He used the 12 disciples of Jesus, who were common working men God chose to do great things.

God gave this simple man a big job to do. When Amos served as a prophet, the people of God had been divided into two nations for more than 150 years. The southern nation was known as **Judah**, and the northern nation was still known as **Israel**. Through the period of the divided monarch Judah saw a succession of kings, some godly and some ungodly (**Uzziah** was one of the better kings of Judah). The northern nation of **Israel** saw nothing but a succession of wicked kings. **Jeroboam the son of Joash** was one of the better kings among these wicked men (especially in a political and military sense) but he was still an ungodly man (2 Kings 14:23-29).

For most of its history, the northern kingdom of Israel struggled against Syria - her neighbor to the north. But around the year 800, the mighty Assyrian Empire defeated Syria, and neutralized this power that hindered Israel's expansion and prosperity. With Syria in check, Israel enjoyed great prosperity during the reign of Jeroboam II.

Do you see the picture? God called a simple farmer to preach to a prosperous nation who had forgotten Him. We might think that the successful times needed a sophisticated preacher, a smooth talker who graduated from a top theological academy. Yet God had other plans. God knew that He could use this unlikely man in a great way.

Perhaps it is time for you start thinking outside the box. Perhaps you have thought that God could only use you in ways that seem logical and reasonable. God can and will use you in ways that makes sense; but you need to also think outside that box, considering that the most important qualification is the call of God. Not only *can* God use humble people like Amos, He *specializes* in it. Remember the principle: *God resists the proud, but gives grace to the humble* (1 Peter 5:5).

WEIGHING GOD DOWN

Behold, I am weighed down by you, as a cart full of sheaves is weighed down. Therefore flight shall perish from the swift, the strong shall not strengthen his power, nor shall the mighty deliver himself.
(Amos 2:13-14)

A common idea in the Psalms is that we can and should bless the LORD. Of course, we can't bless God in the sense that a greater being bestows a blessing on a lesser being, because God is the greater and we are the lesser. In that sense He blesses us and we cannot bless Him. Yet in the Psalms the idea is used in a different way, with the sense that we bless God by worshipping Him and pleasing Him. We bless Him by *being* a blessing unto Him without worship, our words, and our life. It's a beautiful idea that we can *bless God* in this way.

You might say that the Prophet Amos here gives the exact opposite. Instead of being a blessing to God, Amos spoke for the LORD and told God's people that they were a *weight* to Him. It's right there in Amos 2:13: "**I am weighed down by you.**" In the days of the Prophet Amos, God regarded the people of Israel as a weary burden and not as a joy. It is like the difference between the pleasure a parent feels in dealing with an obedient child and the drudgery a parent feels in dealing with a stubborn, rebellious child.

When we read a passage like this, we understand that Amos speaks in figures of speech. We can't say that men oppress God. We shouldn't think that God paces the throne room of heaven, full of worry. In the words of Charles Spurgeon, we know that "all the sin that man can commit can never disturb the serenity of his perfections, nor cause so much as a wave upon the sea of his everlasting calm." Yet we appreciate that Amos speaks to us in the manner of men, telling us that God can be so pressed by the sin of man, especially the sins of His people, as if He were **weighed down** by them.

Any time justice is perverted - any time the rich receive preferential treatment, or the poor are oppressed - it burdens the God who sees from heaven and He promises to set it right. Any time people cheat and manipulate and make money off of others in questionable ways - even if it is legal - it burdens the God who sees from heaven and He promises to set it right. Any time people unfairly profit at the expense of the unfortunate, it burdens the God who sees from heaven and He promises to set it right.

What will God do with this weight? He will eventually, after much patience and longsuffering, bring judgment against those who have weighed Him down. That's what Amos means in verse 14: **"Flight shall perish from the swift, the strong shall not strengthen his power."** One way the judgment of God would express itself against Israel was that they would find themselves unable to succeed in ways they previously thought they were strong.

Without the blessing of God, **the swift** isn't fast enough, **the strong** isn't strong enough, and **the mighty** isn't mighty enough to succeed. Israel was far too confident in their own ability, but God would bring them low.

We can escape this judgment by realizing *now* that even our strength is nothing without God. Paul communicated this idea in 1 Corinthians 10:12: *Therefore let him who thinks he stands take heed lest he fall.* We can become more vulnerable in our perceived *strengths* than in our acknowledged *weaknesses*, because we are on guard with our weaknesses.

The better way is to never let it get to that place of judgment by never weighing God down. Instead of pressing a burden on God by disobedience and mistreatment of others, be a blessing to Him today.

TWENTY-ONE
Bible Reading: Amos 3

LEARNING FROM OTHERS

"Hear and testify against the house of Jacob," says the Lord GOD, the God of hosts, "That in the day I punish Israel for their transgressions, I will also visit destruction on the altars of Bethel; and the horns of the altar shall be cut off and fall to the ground. I will destroy the winter house along with the summer house; the houses of ivory shall perish, and the great houses shall have an end," says the LORD.
(Amos 3:13-15)

Amos was a prophet with a social conscience. This sheepherder from ancient Israel looked at the greed and materialism that marked his age and spoke out boldly against the rich who oppressed the poor and promised God would judge them for their greed.

In these few verses, we see that God wanted ancient Israel to know that this promised judgment was *certain*. Many people think that God is righteous and will judge the world – or at least judge *others* for their sin. For ourselves, we can think of many reasons why God would or should excuse our sins. It is far too easy to think that we are exceptions to the rule.

It is easy to think that because we perform some religious ceremony that we will be spared judgment. Think of a greedy, selfish man who cheats and steals to gain and maintain his wealth. The greedy man tells himself that God gives him a free pass on such sins because he regularly attends church. "God is pleased by my religious observance," he thinks. But he is blind to the fact that a religious veneer can not cover over a corrupt life.

That is just the point the prophet Amos made when he announced on God's behalf, "**I will also visit destruction on the altars of Bethel; and the horns of the altar shall be cut off and fall to the ground**." The greedy in ancient Israel found refuge in their religious observance, but God saw right through it. They would not find refuge in their idol worship. Instead, the altars of dedication to idols would be destroyed by God's judgment. When we build a place of idolatry, we invite God to destroy it.

It's also easy to think that because we have wealth and material things that we are exempt from God's judgment. The greedy man looks at his big house and his fancy car and believes that somehow these things insulate him from the troubles others endure. He tells himself that his material prosperity is God's mark of approval and that it is his security against a coming calamity. To these greedy men who trusted in their wealth, God said through Amos: "**The great houses shall have an end**." God's judgment would not stop at places of idol worship; it would also extend to places built and enjoyed through oppression and robbery.

We live in a very greedy and materialistic age, but most of us think that we could never be judged for such things. Perhaps you think that you can't be so greedy or materialistic because you are not rich. But poor people can be just as greedy as rich people. It's a matter of the heart much more than a matter of the bank account. It is important to learn from the warnings that others received, instead of only learning from our own judgment.

In 2004, during an attempt to set a world record for deep diving, Australian David Shaw reached the amazing depth of 271 meters in the Boesmansgat sinkhole in South Africa. Down that far, he made a shocking discovery: he was not the first one there. At those great depths he found the skeletal remains of Deon Dreyer, who had never come up from a similar record-setting attempt in 1994. Shaw said he could have gone deeper, but gave up his quest after he found Dreyer's body.

Smart man. He learned from the bad experience of someone else. In the same way, we should learn from God's warning to the greedy and materialistic people in ancient Israel through the Prophet Amos. We should get right with God now because we can't find refuge in religious appearance or in our own material success.

TWENTY-TWO
Bible Reading: Amos 4

WARNING THE FAT COWS

Hear this word, you cows of Bashan, who are on the mountain of Samaria, who oppress the poor, who crush the needy, who say to your husbands, "Bring wine, let us drink!" (Amos 4:1)

This man Amos wasn't trained as a prophet, and it is no more evident than right here. This simple man knew farms and fields and flocks instead of the vocabulary of the professional prophets. Therefore when he wanted to get the point across to the indulgent women of ancient Israel, he called them *fat cows*. It's right there when he said to them, "**You cows of Bashan**."

The livestock of **Bashan** - in the northern part of Israel, the modern-day Golan Heights - was known for being fat and healthy. Psalm 22:12 mentions the *strong bulls of Bashan*; Ezekiel 39:18 mentions the large livestock, the *fatlings of Bashan*. It's no exaggeration to say that Amos calls these women "fat cows."

This wasn't primarily a comment on their *appearance*. Amos had no interest in beauty contests, and he wasn't trying to make these women of ancient Israel feel unattractive physically, but he wanted them to see just what their own self-indulgent selfishness made them. Yet don't think that the women liked being called "**Cows of Bashan**." Even though it is true that the very skinny ideal of female beauty is a modern phenomenon, and that especially in ancient times plumpness was a valued sign of affluence, we can count on it that at no time in human history has a woman appreciated being called a *fat cow*.

So when Amos used the sarcastic taunt, "**You cows of Bashan**," he focused on the luxury that these wealthy women of ancient Israel enjoyed and to the self-indulgent and comfort-worshipping ways that their extravagant life-style made possible. In our modern world, we might say that if Amos looked at some desperate women, even if their figures were thin he would call out to them, "**You cows of Bashan**."

Amos saw their opulent, lazy lives, lived for no greater purpose than pleasing self. He saw past the outward shell that they worked so hard to make and keep attractive and see that they were really like fat cows – not only in style and attitude, but also in the fact that they were ready for slaughter.

The point is clear when Amos put his finger on their sins: "**Who oppress the poor, who crush the needy**." The real sin of these ancient women wasn't found in their dress size or in their bank accounts. It was that they gained their wealth and affluence by oppressing and crushing the less fortunate. Perhaps it was because they directly oppressed the poor and crushed the needy. Perhaps it was that their constant demands for luxuries drove their husbands to greater and greater injustices. Perhaps it was a combination of both.

The bossiness of these **cows of Bashan** is shown in how they spoke to their husbands: **Who say to your husbands, "Bring wine, let us drink!"** They used their affluence in the pure, self-focused pursuit of pleasure. God saw this and promised to hold them to account.

God has given you gifts and advantages. How are you using them? Take the tragic lesson from God's message to the **cows of Bashan** to heart: use whatever gifts and advantages God gives you for His glory.

TWENTY-THREE
Bible Reading: Amos 4

PREPARE TO MEET YOUR GOD

Therefore thus will I do to you, O Israel; because I will do this to you, prepare to meet your God, O Israel! For behold, He who forms mountains, and creates the wind, who declares to man what his thought is, and makes the morning darkness, who treads the high places of the earth; the LORD God of hosts is His name.
(Amos 4:12-13)

Amos was a prophet of warning to Israel, warning them to prepare for judgment that was certain if they did not repent. Sensing the hardness of Israel and their refusal to turn back to God, now – inspired by the Spirit of God – Amos took another approach. He simply told them: "**Prepare to meet your God**." We can apply this text in three ways: It is a *challenge*, an *invitation*, and a *summons*

As a *challenge*, God invites His enemies to **prepare to meet** Him. A boxer prepares long and hard before stepping into the ring against a champion. If you are going to step into the ring with God, you had better prepare! It is as if the inspired prophet challenged these proud rebels against God to get ready to meet the God they had rejected and despised.

As an *invitation*, this is a blessing. The invitation God made to Adam, "**Prepare to meet your God**" was nothing but a *blessing* to Adam. Ever since the fall it is our nature to hide from God; therefore the call "**Prepare to meet your God**" has a different sense entirely. Still, if we will come to God we must **prepare** ourselves. When you come to spend time devoted to God – whether by yourself or in the company of others – spend some time preparing yourself first. You would never go into the throne room of a great king without carefully preparing yourself and planning your conduct in His presence. With this thinking, prepare yourself to meet God and be more blessed when in His presence.

As a *summons*, we recognize that one day all will stand before God and give account. Think about just *who* it is that you must meet. You are called one day to a divine appointment, when you must stand for a personal interview before the God of all creation. If you have rejected God, you must stand before the one whose laws you have broken, the one whose penalties you have mocked, the one whose grace you have refused. You will stand before a Being who knows *everything* about you; He has seen your heart, read your thoughts, and remembered every idle word and deed. You will stand before the God who sees through ever veil of hypocrisy and mask of tradition or ceremony. There is no way you can make yourself out to be better than you really are before Him.

Amos ends this section by reminding us who this God is whom we must prepare to meet: "**The LORD God of hosts is His name**." Do you remember the idea behind the title, "**The LORD of hosts**"? "Host" is a military word; in this context it refers to the angelic armies that serve the living God and are at His disposal. But Amos didn't want to just leave it at that. In these two brief verses he tells us a lot more about this great God:

- He is the God of all creation ("**He who forms mountains, and creates the wind**").
- He is the God who is absolutely sovereign over man ("**Who declares to man what his thought is**").
- He is the God with all power over nature ("**And makes the morning darkness**").
- He is the God who rules above all ("**Who treads the high places of the earth**").

Remembering all this reminds us to prepare now and meet this glorious God of grace, so that we do not need to meet Him as a God of judgment at a later time. Prepare to meet your God; prepare to meet Him in a *good* way now so you don't have to meet Him in a *bad* way later.

TWENTY-FOUR

Bible Reading: Amos 5

THE DARK DAY OF THE LORD

Woe to you who desire the day of the LORD! For what good is the day of the LORD to you? It will be darkness, and not light. It will be as though a man fled from a lion, and a bear met him! Or as though he went into the house, leaned his hand on the wall, and a serpent bit him! Is not the day of the LORD darkness, and not light? Is it not very dark, with no brightness in it? (Amos 5:18-20)

Amos was not a professional prophet. God compelled this simple farmer to speak to Israel for two reasons. First, the professional prophets weren't listening to the LORD. Second, the people did not listen to the professional prophets. So God called an untrained man to do a great work at a critical time, a time when Israel stood in the shadow of coming judgment.

It would be a severe judgment. In the few verses before our text, Amos said that the calamity would reach so far that "*they shall call the farmer to mourning, and skillful lamenters to wailing.*" This referred to the ancient Jewish practice of hiring professional mourners to wail at a funeral. Amos described judgment so widespread that there was a shortage of skillful lamenters, so they had to hire the farmer to do the mourning. Just as God used a farmer as a prophet, so judgment would be so bad that farmers would become professional mourners.

In this warning from Amos 5, he confronted the people of Israel: "**For what good is the day of the LORD to you? It will be darkness, and not light**." The day of the LORD is a familiar theme throughout the Bible. The term **day of the LORD** (used more than 25 times in the Bible) does not necessarily refer to one specific day; it speaks of "God's time." The idea is that now is the *day of man*, but the day of man will not last forever. One day, the Messiah will end the day of man and bring forth the **day of the LORD**.

In their religious ritualism, Israel still claimed they longed for **the day of the LORD**. It would be like a person today who said they wanted Jesus to come back real soon, but they lived in a way that wasn't ready. Such people really don't know what they are asking for, and they don't realize that the day of the LORD will not be easy and nice for everyone. The return of Jesus is a blessing for those who are ready, but it is a curse for those who are not.

Amos rightly warned them that they didn't know what they asked for because **the day of the LORD** would bring them judgment, not mercy. They would end up worse off than before. It **will be as though a man fled from a lion, and a bear met him!** Think of a man running from a lion, and being relieved that he escaped – only to find that a *worse* threat waited for him, namely that **a bear met him**. Or imagine that a man takes rest by leaning against the wall in his own home, and instead of finding rest he finds a snakebite. Or imagine that when the night is done and it is time for the sun to rise, it just gets darker – and all one can say is, "**Is it not very dark, with no brightness in it?**"

Don't be confused. Amos isn't saying that the Day of the LORD *will* be darkness; rather that it will *seem* like darkness to those who are not ready. The bottom line is this: When we are right with God, we *want* **the day of the LORD**. We long for Him to show His strength because we know that we abide in Him. When we are not right with God, we *dread* **the day of the LORD** (or at least we *should* dread it), because when God shows Himself strong His strength may work *against* us. In Joel's day Judah was not right with God, so **the day of the LORD** would be **darkness, and not a light** to them.

Many Christians have a warm anticipation of the return of Jesus, and look forward to the time when the day of man is over and the Day of the LORD shines in full strength. Through the centuries, Amos speaks to us today: do you have good reason to welcome the Day of the LORD? Will it be darkness or light to you?

TWENTY-FIVE
Bible Reading: Amos 6

AT EASE IN ZION

Woe to you who are at ease in Zion, and trust in Mount Samaria,
notable persons in the chief nation, to whom the house of Israel comes!
Go over to Calneh and see; and from there go to Hamath the great;
then go down to Gath of the Philistines. Are you better than these
kingdoms? Or is their territory greater than your territory?
(Amos 6:1-2)

In these verses from Amos 6, the prophet compared Israel to her pagan neighbors. He listed the names of ancient kingdoms that are mostly forgotten to us today, but were well-known in the time of Amos. The prophet warned them that if they continued in the same rejection of God, they would end up in the same place as these forgotten kingdoms. The danger of Israel's rebellion made it wrong for them to relax – therefore Amos warned them, "**Woe to you who are at ease in Zion**." We can relate to this today. In her pride and indulgence, all Israel sought was **ease**. This indulgent lust for comfort and luxury is a sin, and God promised that He would judge ancient Israel for it.

We should remember that the idea of rest isn't all bad. Jesus wants to give us rest (Matthew 11:28-29). There is a rest waiting for the people of God (Hebrews 4:9-11). There is rest for us in heaven (Revelation 4:9-11). Yet, there is another kind of rest, a sinful kind of rest - connected to indifference, laziness, and indulgence.

This is what Amos spoke of. It isn't the confidence of a man who is pardoned, but the ease of a hardened criminal who has learned to despise the law. It is not the assurance of one who stands on the rock, but the ease of a senseless drunkard, whose house shakes on its sandy foundations, and yet he parties at full speed. It is not the calm of soul at peace with God, but the ease of a madman who thinks that because he hides his sin from his own eyes, he also thinks he has concealed it from God.

How did this sinful **ease** of God's people show itself?

• It was shown in *presumption*, because they trusted in the might of Mount Samaria.

• It was shown in *procrastination*, because they *put far off the day of doom* (Amos 6:3).

• It was shown in *cruelty to men*, because they caused *the seat of violence to come near* (Amos 6:3).

• It was shown in *love of self*, through all the self-indulgence described in Amos 6:4-6.

• It was shown in *carelessness*, in the willful, drunken ignorance of Amos 6:6.

We say it all the time to each other – "Take it easy!" We should remember that there is a good way to take it easy and a bad way. The good way finds refuge in Jesus and a rest in Him that leads to productive labor for the Kingdom of God. The bad way to "take it easy" is rooted in simple self-indulgence.

At the end of Amos 6:2, God asked Israel a challenging question. He wanted them to look at the kingdoms that time would forget and ask, "**Are you better than these kingdoms?**" God wanted to rebuke the pride of Israel by making them compare themselves to some of their pagan neighbors. Perhaps they weren't so great after all. Perhaps these cities already suffered the judgment of God, and God wanted ancient Israel to know that they would be judged next because they were no better than those kingdoms and enjoyed a sinful ease instead of a righteous rest.

Don't get trapped in the enjoyment of a sinful ease.

TWENTY-SIX
Bible Reading: Amos 7

USING ORDINARY PEOPLE

Then Amos answered, and said to Amaziah: "I was no prophet, nor was I a son of a prophet, but I was a sheepbreeder and a tender of sycamore fruit. Then the LORD took me as I followed the flock, and the LORD said to me, 'Go, prophesy to My people Israel.'"
(Amos 7:14-15)

Amaziah was a professional priest, presiding over the idolatrous worship center the northern kingdom of Israel established at Bethel. Since he was on the government payroll, he sent a message to his boss – Jeroboam, King of Israel – warning the king against this upstart prophet named Amos. Amaziah accused Amos of taking part in a conspiracy to bring down King Jeroboam, and the professional prophet-for-pay told Amos to shut up and go back to Judah.

Amos was not a graduate of the school of the prophets. He was more familiar with the plow than with the pulpit. He knew more about seeds and sowing than seeing into the future. He came right out and said it: "**I was no prophet, nor was I a son of a prophet**." When faced with the accusation of masterminding a conspiracy, Amos replied to Amaziah by noting that he was a reluctant, unprofessional prophet - only a farmer by trade. Amos was hardly the type to launch a conspiracy.

It seems that Amos was simply doing his job as a farmer when one day it happened: "**Then the LORD took me as I followed the flock**." Like many others in the Bible, God called Amos as he faithfully performed his present calling. It was because Amos was an honorable "**sheepbreeder and a tender of sycamore fruit**" that God made him an honorable prophet.

We should not think that the life of Amos as useless as a "**sheepbreeder and a tender of sycamore fruit**" until God called him to serve as a prophet. The world needs sheepbreeders and farmers and mechanics and doctors and technicians and insurance salesmen and consultants and everything else, and to serve God and others honorably in these professions is just as honorable as serving Him as a prophet. Don't think that you can only serve God well in a "ministry" position; do what you do as unto the Lord and every honorable profession is a glorious calling.

At the same time, we see also that God had a purpose in specifically calling a man like Amos. He wanted to show that the greatness of the ministry was in the God who inspires it, not in the man or woman used in ministry. It is as Paul said in 2 Corinthians 4:7: "*But we have this treasure in earthen vessels, that the excellence of the power may be of God and not of us.*" When Amos spoke people didn't say, "He sure learned his lessons well at the school of the prophets." Instead they said, "God is really saying something through that farmer."

God had another purpose in calling Amos; He used Amos *as* a "**sheepbreeder and a tender of sycamore fruit.**" With so many allusions and illustrations from the world of agriculture, Amos spoke as a farmer and God used it. Every person that is really called to speak forth for God has a manner and style of their own. Although God speaks through them all, they still do not lose their individuality or originality of personality. We might say that the breath which causes the music is the same, but no two instruments give forth precisely the same sound. Amos was a unique instrument and God breathed through him in a special way.

You, dear reader, are a unique individual. You are singular in both what you are by birth and by life experience. God can and will use you according to your special calling. It may be in a way noticed or unnoticed by others, but that is unimportant – as long as your calling is noticed in heaven. Just make sure that you answer when He calls.

TWENTY-SEVEN
Bible Reading: Amos 8

FEAST OR FAMINE?

"Behold, the days are coming," says the Lord GOD, "That I will send a famine on the land, not a famine of bread, nor a thirst for water, but of hearing the words of the LORD. They shall wander from sea to sea, and from north to east; they shall run to and fro, seeking the word of the LORD, but shall not find it." (Amos 8:11-12)

We see the pictures from time to time – heart rending pictures of thousands of people suffering under the tragedy of famine. In such desperate times, the world often mobilizes to bring food to these troubled regions, and often disaster is prevented from becoming a catastrophe.

The Prophet Amos reminds us that there is another kind of famine: "**I will send a famine on the land, not a famine of bread, nor a thirst for water, but of hearing the words of the LORD.**" Notice carefully the nature of this **famine**. It is not a lack of God's Word, but a **famine...of *hearing* the words of the LORD**. It isn't that God's Word isn't available, but that it is not listened to. It is not a case of God withholding His revelation; but of people being in such a state that they do not see it, they do not hear the words.

It is true that there may be times where there is a famine of God's Word, either through the neglect or the unfaithfulness of those who have the responsibility to present God's Word. But that isn't what Amos meant here. This is a problem with the *hearer*, not with the *preacher*. The preacher may have his own problems to deal with and to answer for before God; but the hearer may have his own problems also.

1 Thessalonians 2:13 describes the right way to hear the Word of God: "*When you received the word of God which you heard from us, you welcomed it not as the word of men, but as it is in truth, the*

word of God, which also effectively works in you who believe." They received the word, they welcomed the word, they regarded it as the word of God, and they allowed it to work effectively in their life. That is effective hearing.

Amos continued his warning: "**They shall wander...seeking the word of the LORD, but they shall not find it**." When we push away God's Word for a long time, we may find ourselves in the place were we **shall not find it** even if we wanted to. This makes us remember that the ability to hear God's Word and to *benefit* by it is a gift from God, and it is a gift that should not to be despised.

Jesus alluded to this principle in a parable: "*Take heed what you hear. With the same measure you use, it will be measured to you; and to you who hear, more will be given. For whoever has, to him more will be given; but whoever does not have, even what he has will be taken away from him.*" (Mark 4:24-25) When we seek God, it generally becomes easier to find Him. When we push away God, it generally becomes more difficult to hear and to receive His Word.

Is there famine in your life right now? Perhaps you find it easy to blame the pastor or the preacher, and you think that if they only preached better sermons, you would enjoy a great spiritual feast. But have you looked at your own life, your own attitude? Perhaps the famine in your life is a famine of *hearing*, and the problem is with you. You owe it to yourself to seek God on the matter. It would be terrible to stay in a problem and to blame others when the problem is really with you.

Since it is true that *man does not live by bread alone, but by every word that proceeds from the mouth of God* (Matthew 4:4), then it is true that a famine of hearing God's Word can be as catastrophic in a spiritual sense as a famine of bread is a disaster for the world. The bread is out there – get your hearing right and enjoy the feast.

TWENTY-EIGHT
Bible Reading: Amos 9

PLOWMAN AND REAPER

"Behold, the days are coming," says the LORD, "When the plowman shall overtake the reaper, and the treader of grapes him who sows seed; the mountains shall drip with sweet wine, and all the hills shall flow with it." (Amos 9:13)

The Book of Amos is filled with many strong warnings to God's people. In their prosperity they forgot God, but God did not forget them. He sent prophets like the simple farmer Amos to turn the people back. God knew that they would not turn back and He said so through Amos. Nevertheless, God would not abandon His failing people, and He promised an ultimate restoration. Here, in the rich images that came easily to a farmer like Amos, God promised remarkable reinvigoration of the nation.

He announced that "**The days are coming**" and under God's inspiration, the prophet Amos ended his words to the nation on this note of high hope, looking forward to a day of great prosperity and abundance in Israel. Under the reign of Jeroboam II, they *had* material abundance, but not in the LORD. God promised to restore them to prosperity *from Him* and *in Him*.

Indeed, the days would come "**When the plowman shall overtake the reaper**." With this phrase, Amos described how miraculous and amazing God's blessing and restoration would be.

First, when God releases blessing and restoration, fruit comes *quickly*. Normally, the **plowman** and the **reaper** work apart, their effort separated by many months. But under these unique seasons of blessing and restoration, they bump into each other. The crops were so big that the **plowman** and the **reaper** didn't have time to let the other finish their work. We should pray for such seasons of quick fruit.

We also see that when God releases blessing and restoration, fruit comes from *unexpected places*. Normally, grapevines don't grow well on mountains or high hills where the weather is a problem, but in the days of Israel's restoration even "**the mountains shall drip with sweet wine and all the hills shall flow with it**." We should pray for such seasons of unexpected fruit.

When God releases blessing and restoration, fruit comes with great quality. Amos looked forward to the day when the wine that came quickly and from unexpected places would be **sweet wine**. Without being a wine connoisseur, Amos used this phrase to describe *good* and *high quality* fruit from the work. We should pray for such seasons of good fruit.

When God releases blessing and restoration, the work is blessed - but it is still *work*. The **plowman**, the **reaper**, the **treader of grapes**, and **him who sows seed** still had their work to do. God doesn't just do it all for them, but under God's blessing and restoration the work is done with energy and joy. The **plowman** doesn't just wait around; he gets busy even if he starts bumping into the **reaper**! These seasons of unexpected blessing do not mean that God's people sit on their hands and do nothing. There is still work for the **plowman** and the **reaper**, but it is glorious, blessed work.

Even when we are *not* in such blessed times, the work of God deserves our energy and effort. We don't work for God only when it seems glorious, but even when it is more difficult. We are ready in season and out of season. Yet without apology we look forward to and enjoy special seasons of God's blessing – and we should especially pray for them.

TWENTY-NINE
Bible Reading: Obadiah

DOING RIGHT IN THE DAY OF DISTRESS

You should not have entered the gate of My people in the day of their calamity. Indeed, you should not have gazed on their affliction in the day of their calamity, nor laid hands on their substance in the day of their calamity. You should not have stood at the crossroads to cut off those among them who escaped; nor should you have delivered up those among them who remained in the day of distress.
(Obadiah 12-14)

The Book of Obadiah is certainly one of the more hidden books of the Bible; most people know nothing of its message and might have a bit of trouble making sense of it all. If we want to make sense of Obadiah, we need to first understand the context of the book.

Obadiah's prophecy is unique because he doesn't deal with Judah or Israel much at all. His focus is on the sin of Edom and the judgment coming upon them. The Edomites are the people descended from Esau, the son of Isaac and Rebekah and the brother of Jacob (Genesis 25:19-34). Esau was nicknamed "Edom" (which means, "red") probably because he had red hair. The nations of Edom and Israel existed side by side through many centuries, some times cooperative and sometimes competitive.

Obadiah wrote of a time when Judah was attacked and the Edomites did nothing to help them – worse yet, they *rejoiced* in the calamity that came upon Israel and they profited themselves by it. Edom should have helped because of the family connection. But when enemies attacked Judah, Edom did nothing. They stood by and cheered for Judah's misery. Sometimes doing *nothing* is a great sin. Numbers 32:23 speaks of the sin that *will find you out*, and the sin it speaks of is the sin of doing *nothing*.

Yet Edom actually did worse than nothing; they **rejoiced** over another's misfortune and suffering and used it as an occasion to exalt themselves (**nor should you have spoken proudly in the day of distress**).

Then their sin became worse: Edom's sin started with doing *nothing*, then progressed to *pride* over Judah's distress. Soon, they took advantage of their brother Judah's misfortune and **laid hands on their substance**.

The final progression of Edom's sin was worst of all - they joined in the attack against vulnerable Judah (**You should not have stood at the crossroads to cut off those among them who escaped**). When they encountered people from Judah fleeing southward from the attacking army, they killed them (**cut off**) or gave them over to the enemy as prisoners (**delivered up those among them who remained**).

Obadiah repeats it like the chorus to a tragic song: **In the day of his captivity...in the day of distress...in the day of calamity**. All in all, Edom treated God's people terribly when **distress** and **calamity** came upon them. For all this, God's judgment was coming upon them.

- First they did nothing.
- Then they rejoiced in their distress and calamity.
- Then they took advantage of their vulnerable state.
- Then they joined in the violence against God's people.

Are we guilty of the same - or worse - when we see others in **distress** or **calamity**? Do we take advantage of or profit from calamity in the life of others? If so, God sees it as sin and He must deal with it in our life. Invite Him to do it, and do right in the day of someone else's distress.

THIRTY
Bible Reading: Jonah 1

IMPULSE, CIRCUMSTANCES, OR GOD?

But Jonah arose to flee to Tarshish from the presence of the LORD. He went down to Joppa, and found a ship going to Tarshish; so he paid the fare, and went down into it, to go with them to Tarshish from the presence of the LORD. (Jonah 1:3)

God gave Jonah a job to do, but he didn't want any part of it. It's not a stretch to think that Jonah knew the job would be difficult and was intimidated. Nahum 3:1-4 gives us a good idea of how wicked the people of Nineveh were. Jonah had every reason to expect that at the very best, he would be mocked and treated as a fool. He might be attacked and killed if he did what the LORD told him to do.

Nevertheless, for Jonah it was more than an issue of difficulty. It was also because Jonah didn't *want* the Assyrians in Nineveh to escape God's judgment. Imagine a Jewish man in New York during World War II hearing God say, "I'm going to bring terrible judgment on Germany. I want you to go to Berlin and tell Nazi Germany to repent." Instead of doing it, the man heads for San Francisco and then hops on a boat for Hong Kong. Tarshish was in exactly the opposite direction as Nineveh.

We don't doubt that Jonah *felt* like going to Tarshish. There was an impulse within him driving him there, but it was a dangerous impulse. We may take Jonah as an example of the danger of doing things under mere impulse instead of the guidance of the Holy Spirit.

• An impulse may be *very brave*, yet wrong (Jonah was very brave in embarking on such a long sea-journey).

• An impulse may appear to be *self-denying*, yet wrong (it cost Jonah much in money and comfort to go on this long sea-journey).

- An impulse may *lay claim to freedom*, yet be wrong (wasn't Jonah "free" to go to Nineveh?).
- An impulse may lead someone to do *something that they would condemn in others* (what would Jonah say to another prophet disobeying God?).
- An impulse can make us do to God or others *what we would never want to be done to ourself.*

Many people take their inner impulses and say, "The Lord told me this or that." This is dangerous even when it doesn't seem so immediately. "What have you to do with the devices and desires of your own hearts? Are these to be a law to you? I pray you, be not among the foolish ones who will be carried about with every wind of fancy and perversity. 'To the law and to the testimony,' should be your cry, and you may not appeal to inward movements and impulses." (Spurgeon)

Jonah might have even thought that the LORD was guiding him through circumstances. After all, he got the money and paid the fare. This shows the danger of being guided only by *circumstances*. If circumstances are for us or against us, we must let God's Word be our guide. It is very easy to interpret circumstances any way you want to. If we are set on a wrong course, it is no problem for the devil and our deceitful heart to work together and interpret circumstances so that they say whatever we want to hear.

Nevertheless, Jonah paid the fare. When you run away from the LORD, you never get to where you intend to go and you always pay your own fare. When you go the LORD's way, you not only get to where you are going, but He pays the fare. Let God's Word map out your itinerary, not only impulses or circumstances - and let Him pay the fare!

THIRTY-ONE
Bible Reading: Jonah 1

ASLEEP IN THE STORM

Then the mariners were afraid; and every man cried out to his god, and threw the cargo that was in the ship into the sea, to lighten the load. But Jonah had gone down into the lowest parts of the ship, had lain down, and was fast asleep. So the captain came to him, and said to him, "What do you mean, sleeper? Arise, call on your God; perhaps your God will consider us, so that we may not perish." (Jonah 1:5-6)

The thought of an exhausted Jesus sleeping in the boat on the stormy Sea of Galilee is touching. The thought of rebellious, disobedient Jonah asleep in the boat is not. What a curious and tragic scene! All the sailors were religious men, devout in prayer to their gods. Yet their gods were really *nothing*, and could do *nothing*. There was one man on board who had a relationship with the true God, who knew His Word, and who worshipped Him - *yet he was asleep!*

The same irony confronts sleeping Christians today. With the storms whipped up by the world, the flesh, and devil there is no proper place for a sleeping Christian. Yet still some are like Jonah and have no problem sleeping while the storm rages around them and lives hang in the balance. The nature of Jonah's sleep can teach us, because it is all too much like the sleep of the careless Christian:

- Jonah slept in a place where he hoped no one would see him or disturb him, and sleeping Christians like to "hide out" among the church.
- Jonah slept in a place where he could not help with the work that needed to be done, and sleeping Christians stay away from the work of the LORD.
- Jonah slept while there was a prayer meeting up on the deck. Sleeping Christians don't like prayer meetings.

- Jonah slept and had no idea of the problems around him. Sleeping Christians don't know what is really going on.
- Jonah slept when he was in great danger. Sleeping Christians are in danger, but don't know it.
- Jonah slept while the heathen needed him. Sleeping Christians snooze on while the world needs their message and testimony.

Some - if not most - sleeping Christians protest that they are not asleep at all.

- "We talk about Jesus" - but you can *talk* in your sleep.
- "We have a walk for Jesus" - but you can *walk* in your sleep.
- "We have passion for Jesus - I wept in a time of worship just the other day" - but you can *cry* in your sleep.
- "We have joy and rejoice in Jesus" - but you can *laugh* in your sleep.
- "We think about Jesus all the time" - but you can *think* while you are asleep; we call it *dreaming*.

You can know if you are spiritually asleep or not. Perhaps the best way to know if you are fully awake is to measure your life and see if you live with a true, thorough consciousness of spiritual things. Are heaven and hell *real* to you, or are they just abstract ideas? Is the soul of another person less real than their physical form? Truly awake Christians live with full and proper awareness of the things that really matter, the things of eternity. They think and act in light of eternal matters, not transient shadows and dreams.

Perhaps it is time for us to hear what the ship captain said to Jonah: "What do you mean, sleeper? Arise, call on your God." Ask God to make you fully awake.

THIRTY-TWO
Bible Reading: Jonah 1

AFRAID AND MORE AFRAID

Therefore they cried out to the LORD and said, "We pray, O LORD, please do not let us perish for this man's life, and do not charge us with innocent blood; for You, O LORD, have done as it pleased You." So they picked up Jonah and threw him into the sea, and the sea ceased from its raging. Then the men feared the LORD exceedingly, and offered a sacrifice to the LORD and took vows. (Jonah 1:14-16)

It was a perfectly dreadful storm for the sailors on the ship headed to Tarshish. This storm was so fierce, so dark, and so evil that they knew it was more than a storm. It was the judgment of God upon them all, or at least upon one on board. Every man cried out to his god with unmatched fervor, knowing that only a miracle from the heavens could save them - or at least *almost* every man cried out. They found one sleepy stowaway, dragged him to the deck and asked him to pray to his God. Then someone had the idea - perhaps the wrath of God is upon only one of us, and that one must pay for their sin so that the whole ship can be saved. Drawing straws, the short straw ended up in the hand of the sleepy stowaway. They asked him his story and found out he was a prophet on the run from the living God.

At that point, Jonah did a very brave thing. He offered to sacrifice himself for the sake of the perishing men on board the ship. "Throw me in - let me bear the wrath of God and the sea, and you will be spared." To their credit, the sailors wouldn't do it. Instead, they rowed harder than ever against the violence of the storm, but the storm answered back with greater force than ever. The sailors did not want to throw Jonah into the sea because they believed his God was real and they dreaded the consequences of throwing a prophet - even a disobedient prophet - into the sea. Still, when all hope seemed to be lost they took precautions ("**We pray, O LORD, please do not let**

us perish for this man's life, and do not charge us with innocent blood") and threw Jonah into the sea.

Instantly, everything changed. **The sea ceased from its raging**. The immediate end of the storm proved that Jonah's God was real, and his resistance was the real problem. In a logical response the sailors **feared the LORD exceedingly**, sacrificed to God and made promises to serve Him. The sailors moved from fearing the storm to fearing the LORD.

Indeed, we can see a pattern that illustrates the salvation of every needy sinner when we examine the actions of the crew on this ship bound for Tarshish.

- Sinners, when they are tossed upon the sea of conviction, make desperate efforts to save themselves.
- The fleshly efforts of awakened sinners must inevitably fail.
- The soul's sorrow will continue to increase as long as it relies on its own efforts.
- The way of safety for sinners is to be found in the sacrifice of another on their behalf.

In a wonderful sermon on this passage, Charles Spurgeon said: "Brethren, I wish I had adequate words to fitly describe the peace which comes to a human heart when we learn to see Jesus cast into the sea of divine wrath on our account. Conscience accuses no longer. Judgment now decides for the sinner instead of against him. Memory can look back upon past sins, with sorrow for the sin it is true, but yet with no dread of any penalty to come. It is a blessed thing for a man to know that he cannot be punished, that heaven and earth may shake, but he cannot be punished for his sin."

You should know that blessing, and you should want others to know it. You should know that the sacrifice of another on your behalf has turned away the wrath of God. If you have received it, then by all means enjoy it as God's most precious gift to you and an enduring proof of His love.

THIRTY-THREE
Bible Reading: Jonah 2

REPENTED - AND STILL REPENTING

"Those who regard worthless idols forsake their own Mercy. But I will sacrifice to You with the voice of thanksgiving; I will pay what I have vowed. Salvation is of the LORD." (Jonah 2:8-9)

We don't really know what it was like for Jonah in the belly of the fish, but it probably wasn't pleasant. In the Disney animated feature Pinocchio, Gepeto and Pinocchio didn't have it so bad inside of Monstro - they had a nice little raft with a crate for a table and a candle stuck into an old bottle for light. It's safe to say that Jonah didn't have it so nice, yet it was a good place for him nonetheless. It was in the belly of the fish that Jonah prayed this great prayer and received deliverance from the LORD.

In his prayer, Jonah finally realized that resisting God or running from Him was like being an idolater. He said in his prayer, "**Those who regard worthless idols forsake their own Mercy**." In the belly of the fish he came to his senses and stopped forsaking the LORD who was his Mercy. Now he said, "**But I will sacrifice to You**." Jonah repented from running away from God, and he turned to God with sacrifice and thanksgiving. He will pay his vows to God, and do what ever God told him to do. At one time or another, Jonah had probably said what many of us say in the Christian life: "Lord, I'll do what ever You want me to do." Now Jonah realizes fully that he must stop resisting God and he should pay his vows to God.

In the culmination of his prayer, Jonah cried out: "**Salvation is of the LORD**." This was more than a statement of fact; it was Jonah's triumphant declaration. God has saved and will save, and Jonah meant it *personally*. *Jonah's* **salvation is of the LORD**. Jonah knew this in the *close-up* picture; he knew that *his* **salvation is of the LORD**. He also now knew it in the *big picture*; that salvation is not of a nation or a race or a language, or not of man at all. No, **salvation is of the LORD**.

At the end of Jonah's prayer in the belly of the fish, it is clear that Jonah repented, but we might wonder *when* did Jonah repent? It is hard to say exactly when, but there are indications of repentance when...

• Jonah said he feared the LORD and was honest about his story (Jonah 1:9). This was an indication of repentance.

• Jonah allowed himself to be cast into the sea (Jonah 1:12). This was an indication of repentance, casting himself totally on the LORD.

• Jonah called out to God during the three days and three nights in the belly of the fish (Jonah 2:2, 2:4, and 2:7). This was an indication of repentance.

• Jonah renewed his commitment to his vow (Jonah 2:9). This was another indication of repentance.

So, when did Jonah repent? The answer is found in seeing repentance as more than a one-time event. Though it begins at one time, it must continue and mature. It is an event but it is also a process.

Where are you in repentance? If you have turned to the Lord, keep turning and stay turned.

THIRTY-FOUR
Bible Reading: Jonah 3

GOD OF THE SECOND CHANCE

Now the word of the LORD came to Jonah the second time, saying,
"Arise, go to Nineveh, that great city, and preach to it the message that
I tell you." (Jonah 3:1-2)

God loved Jonah enough to come to him a **second time** with His word. This shows the amazing love of God to His wayward people. Though Jonah did everything he could to resist the first call of God, after Jonah repented God called him again - though God was under no obligation to do it. He did it out of mercy and grace.

This is especially remarkable when we remember how the Book of Jonah began: "Now the word of the LORD came to Jonah the son of Amittai, saying, 'Arise, go to Nineveh, that great city, and cry out against it; for their wickedness has come up before Me.'" (Jonah 1:1-2) Do you see the similarity? First, "Now the word of the LORD came to Jonah." Then, "**Now the word of the LORD came to Jonah a second time**." Thank God for that **second time**!

Many of us who believe God has given us a word to bring to others are especially thankful for that second time - or the one hundred and second time. This is pure grace from God. He has every right to exclude us and never use us again once we blow it, but He is the God of the second chance and the one hundred and second chance.

God was determined to do the work through Jonah, so He did not give up on the reluctant prophet. God is often just this committed to doing His work through a man. Look at it this way: God had a job to get done - preaching to Nineveh. He could have used anything or anyone to do it, but He wanted to use Jonah. If God told us to do the job of reaching a city as great as Nineveh, we would have done it all differently. First, we probably would be paralyzed with despair over the size of the job; but if we made it past that, we would have sat down to carefully devise our plans, dividing the city and the suburbs of Nineveh into missionary districts; we should have needed at least several hundreds, it not thousands, of able ministers. We would figure out the money and buildings needed, make a headquarters, and implement our method to get the job done. Nevertheless, God does things differently. A city needed to be reached, so God raised up one man - and by amazing persistence and amazing grace He made that one man qualified to do the job. It's not that it is wrong for us to plan and organize to the best of our ability, but we must always remember that God has every right and reason to over-ride our planning and organizing and we must remain totally comfortable with His doing that. Sometimes God works completely outside our plan.

Notice what God told Jonah to do the second time: "**Preach to it the message that I tell you**." In Jonah 1, God told the prophet to "cry out against Nineveh" but this time God simply tells Jonah to go there and wait for further instructions. God often works this way, and our flesh often finds it irritating that He does. We want it all spelled out long before we take the first step, but God often doesn't deal with us that way. In fact, the story of Jonah demonstrates why God so often leads us one step at a time without telling us more. When God told Jonah what he would say in Nineveh, Jonah rejected the call. God often only tells us what we can handle at the time.

We commonly thank God for His word and what He shows us. When was the last time you thanked Him for what He *didn't* tell you? Sometimes His greatest kindness is shown by what He doesn't say, because He knows we aren't ready for it. Today, spend some time thanking God for all the second chances He has given you. Then, spend some more time thanking Him for the things He has mercifully *not* revealed to you. Father really does know best.

THIRTY-FIVE
Bible Reading: Jonah 4

ANGRY - BUT IS IT RIGHT?

Then the Lord said, "Is it right for you to be angry?" (Jonah 4:4)

Jonah had results the most ambitious preacher would be proud of - after a short, harsh sermon constantly repeated, a city repented so radically that even their *livestock* got right with God. The merciful hand of the Lord held back the promised punishment, because every warning of coming judgment is an implied invitation to repent. When the people of Nineveh responded to Jonah's preaching, they answered God's invitation to repent.

Even with these impressive results, Jonah wasn't happy. In fact, he was more depressed and angry than ever because God spared the Assyrians of Nineveh. They were infamous for their brutal treatment of other nations, and God's people in Judah and Israel felt some of their terror. To say it simply, Jonah wanted the Ninevites buried under God's judgment and it made him angry that God invited them to repent and they took Him up on the offer.

The persnickety prophet stewed in his anger for a while. He even complained that the burden of living with the spared city of Nineveh was more than his life could bear, and he begged God to take his life (Jonah 4:3). Jonah then heard the word of the Lord again - but this time it was the word of the Lord for him, not for the people of Nineveh. It was a simple question: "**Is it right for you to be angry?**" As Jonah expressed his anger against God, it was good that he was honest about his feelings; nevertheless we shouldn't think for a moment that all of our feelings towards God are justified.

God likes to ask us questions, because they reveal our heart. It also puts us on proper ground before God, because He has every right to question us and we owe Him answers. Think of some of the great questions God asked:

- Where are you? Who told you that you were naked? What is this you have done? (Genesis 3)
- Where is your brother Abel? What have you done? (Genesis 4)
- Why did you despise the word of the LORD by doing what is evil in His eyes? (2 Samuel 12)
- Whom shall I send? Who will go for us? (Isaiah 6)
- Who do you say that I am? (Matthew 16)
- Are you betraying the Son of Man with a kiss? (Luke 22)
- Saul, Saul, why are you persecuting Me? (Acts 9)

Sometimes when others question us we feel offended and act defensive, and wonder just who they think they are to question us. When God asks the questions, we know He has every right to ask - and we know that every question He asks has a loving purpose behind it.

If we are angry against God, He will ask us the same question He asked Jonah: "**Is it right for you to be angry?**" And the answer must always be "No, Lord. All Your ways are right even if I don't understand them." Jonah could have played the role of the spiritual phony and denied that he was angry against God, but that wouldn't help anything. On the other hand, Jonah could have stubbornly held on to his anger and tried to justify it. The right response is to own up to our anger against God and then to humbly yield it to Him. Sometimes we are angry against God, or disappointed in Him, or we doubt His good intentions towards us. It doesn't do any good to pretend those feelings are not there, but at the same time we shouldn't indulge those feelings. Remember that God has never sinned against us at all, and we can trust Him even when we don't understand what He is doing. Then we can thank God for His loving questions.

THIRTY-SIX
Bible Reading: Micah 1

INCURABLE WOUNDS

Therefore I will wail and howl, I will go stripped and naked; I will make a wailing like the jackals and a mourning like the ostriches, for her wounds are incurable. For it has come to Judah; it has come to the gate of my people; to Jerusalem. (Micah 1:8-9)

We know he came from a village named Moresheth, which was about 25 miles southwest of Jerusalem on the border lands between Judah and the Philistines. This man from the country was sent to the city to bring the word of the LORD. We know that he had a strong sense of his own calling as a prophet, and he says so in Micah 3:8. We also know that he spoke to both Samaria (the capital of the Northern Kingdom) and Jerusalem (the capital of the Southern Kingdom).

The latter years of his ministry were under the great reforming king of Judah, Hezekiah; but his earlier years were under two wicked kings of Judah, Jotham and Ahaz. It may be that the effective ministry of Micah during those difficult years laid the groundwork for the fruitful ministry in the better days of Hezekiah's reign.

Those are the bare facts around the life and ministry of this important prophet. Yet our selected verses, Micah 1:8-9, show us the *heart* of a prophet. Knowing that judgment was about to come upon the people of God unless they repented, he couldn't take the news lightly. Instead he said, "**I will wail and howl.**" Micah couldn't prophesy in a dispassionate, detached way. When he saw judgment coming upon his people, it made him **wail and howl** like **the jackals**.

Do you see his heart? Micah didn't just announce judgment and then yawn. He cared so deeply that he wept with God's people. This shows us that the preacher's duty is more than to just announce judgment and to walk away. He has to *care*. Micah could have come against the erring people of God with the unassailable logic of judgment, but many of those who reject a Christian's logic can be won by a Christian's compassionate tears.

What made this prophet cry? He looked at the people of God and saw, "**Her wounds are incurable**." It was like looking at a person with a terminal disease; knowing there will never be any real improvement, and their condition will just grow worse and worse until death. It would almost be better if the judgment had come and passed, but to see it on the horizon with nothing to stop it – knowing that "**Her wounds are incurable**" – was a deep agony for the Prophet Micah.

What made the wounds incurable? We can say that our only **incurable** wounds are the ones we refuse to bring to God. With Him, all things are possible (Luke 18:27), but when we refuse to bring our sin to Him, then our **wounds are incurable**. In Matthew 12, Jesus spoke of an unforgivable sin – blasphemy against the Holy Spirit. Since the work of the Holy Spirit is to bring us to Jesus (John 15:26 among other passages), to finally reject this work of the Holy Spirit is to finally reject Jesus – leaving our wounds **incurable**.

This is both a comfort and a warning. The comfort is in knowing that if we *will* come to Jesus, every wound is curable. All sin can be forgiven and restoration can be made. God is in the business of making all things new (Revelation 21:5). The warning is that there are definitely some wounds that are **incurable** – we can't push away Jesus, have a positive mental attitude, and trust that everything will turn out alright.

Even in the sorrow of this prophet, there is some comfort for us. We can take his sorrow over the incurable wounds of Judah, and let that direct us to the place where our wounds *can* be cured. We can also point others there.

THIRTY-SEVEN
Bible Reading: Micah 2

THE BREAKER

The one who breaks open will come up before them; they will break out, pass through the gate, and go out by it; their king will pass before them, with the LORD at their head." (Micah 2:13)

If you spend some time with the Minor Prophets, you get a feel for a familiar pattern – God warns of coming judgment, pleading with His people to come back in repentance and wanting relationship with Him; then generous promises of restoration, so as not to bring His people to despair and to assure them of His final victory.

That's the familiar context of this wonderful promise at the end of Micah chapter 2. What makes this passage special is the unique title hidden in the verse. You may understand that there are many wonderful titles and names for Jesus found in the Bible, such as:

Apostle, Author and Finisher of our Faith, Bread of Life, Bridegroom, Captain of Our Salvation, Chief Cornerstone, Immanuel, King of Kings, Lion of the Tribe of Judah, Lord of Lords, Lamb of God, Last Adam, Light of the Nations, Man of Sorrows, Mediator, Prince of Peace, Root of David, Son of David, Sun of Righteousness, Word of Life.

Yet this verse contains a special and unique name for our Messiah: "The Breaker." Look at how the Amplified Bible translates Micah 2:13:

The Breaker [the Messiah] will go up before them. They will break through, pass in through the gate and go out through it. And their King will pass on before them, the LORD at their head.

Look also at the New American Standard Version:

The breaker goes up before them;
They break out, pass through the gate, and go out by it.

> *So their king goes on before them,*
> *And the LORD at their head.*

The King James Version also has this idea:

> *The breaker is come up before them: they have broken up, and*
> *have passed through the gate, and are gone out by it: and their*
> *king shall pass before them, and the LORD on the head of them.*

I have a particular liking for how a German translation renders this title. The Schlachter version mentions "Der Durchbrecher" – "The Break-Through One." No matter how you translate it, Micah's thought is not difficult to follow. He saw Jesus here as *The Breaker*. In this office, he is the captain and leader of His people, advancing in front of His flock.

How we need a *Breaker*, a trailblazer in our life! He goes before us like a mighty ice breaker cutting through thick artic ice, clearing a path so that we His people can follow. We could never go forward if He did not break the way for us, but because He has we *can* and *will* go forward. He cuts the trail, He breaks the way, and we His people follow. It means that He has endured the worst, and though following behind is not always easy, it is always possible because every trial or difficulty we face has first been cut through by Him.

Do you see a hard path in front of you? Don't despair. Ask *The Breaker* to go before you and trust Him to do that; then follow behind knowing that as hard as it might be, He has broken the way before you so that you really can follow. Find comfort in this more obscure title of Jesus, and when you need a breakthrough, you know who to go to!

THIRTY-EIGHT
Bible Reading: Micah 3

THE PROPHET THEY LISTENED TO

Her heads judge for a bribe, her priests teach for pay, and her prophets divine for money. Yet they lean on the LORD, and say, "Is not the LORD among us? No harm can come upon us." Therefore because of you Zion shall be plowed like a field, Jerusalem shall become heaps of ruins, and the mountain of the temple like the bare hills of the forest.
(Micah 3:11-12)

Like most of the prophets, Micah fearlessly confronted the corruption of his time. In this chapter, Micah first spoke to the judges, and then to the prophets - now he spoke to the princes, the heads of the house of Jacob. The rulers of Jerusalem were not much better than the rulers of the apostate northern Kingdom of Israel, and they could expect similar judgment unless they repented.

They needed to repent from a lot. Corruption had deeply set in, like bribery among the judges and a mercenary "I'm in it for the money" attitude among the priests and the prophets. Despite this disgraceful state of things, they still made a pretense of trusting God. As Micah said it, **"Yet they lean on the LORD, and say, 'Is not the LORD among us? No harm can come upon us.'"** The leaders of Jerusalem had a false confidence in religious ritual and form. All the while, judgment was appointed for Jerusalem unless they repented.

For anyone who has studied the prophets of the Old Testament, these lines run along familiar tracks. The bold expose of corruption, the fearless call to repentance. But at this point the lines of Micah's ministry begin to run in a different direction: *they actually listened to him.*

The great thing about the Prophet Micah was that he was listened to. Hosea was ignored, and so was Amos. They threw Jeremiah in jail for his prophetic message of coming judgment. In contrast, King Hezekiah and the leadership of Judah *listened* to the Prophet Micah.

Jeremiah 26:17-19 describes how even a hundred years later the impact of Micah was remembered: *Then certain of the elders of the land rose up and spoke to all the assembly of the people, saying: "Micah of Moresheth prophesied in the days of Hezekiah king of Judah, and spoke to all the people of Judah, saying, 'Thus says the LORD of hosts: "Zion shall be plowed like a field, Jerusalem shall become heaps of ruins, And the mountain of the temple Like the bare hills of the forest."' Did Hezekiah king of Judah and all Judah ever put him to death? Did he not fear the LORD and seek the LORD's favor? And the LORD relented concerning the doom which He had pronounced against them. But we are doing great evil against ourselves."*

We get used to the familiar pattern of people rejecting the counsel of the LORD through His messengers, and then carelessly carrying on to a bitter judgment. Yet it doesn't have to end that way. Sometimes the people of God really do listen and respond to the voice of the Spirit and turn back to God and find Him ready to welcome them back with open arms and His transforming grace. Sometimes it really works just like it should.

We can be happy that Micah was the prophet they listened to. He was heard in the days of Hezekiah and a true revival followed. They even listened to him a hundred years later, and the memory of what happened earlier was used of God to spare the life of Jeremiah.

Two things stick out to us from this passage. First, we take heart even in seasons of discouragement. Sometimes our work for God and His people works just like it should. Second, *we* should be those wise enough and humble enough to listen to what God says, even when it is not what we wanted to hear. We can listen to the messengers God sends our way.

THIRTY-NINE
Bible Reading: Micah 4

THE FOUR FREEDOMS

Now it shall come to pass in the latter days that the mountain of the LORD's house shall be established on the top of the mountains, and shall be exalted above the hills; and peoples shall flow to it. Many nations shall come and say, "Come, and let us go up to the mountain of the LORD, to the house of the God of Jacob; He will teach us His ways, and we shall walk in His paths." For out of Zion the law shall go forth, and the word of the LORD from Jerusalem. He shall judge between many peoples, and rebuke strong nations afar off; they shall beat their swords into plowshares, and their spears into pruning hooks; nation shall not lift up sword against nation, neither shall they learn war any more. But everyone shall sit under his vine and under his fig tree, and no one shall make them afraid; for the mouth of the LORD of hosts has spoken. For all people walk each in the name of his god, but we will walk in the name of the LORD our God forever and ever. (Micah 4:1-5)

In 1941 President Franklin Roosevelt gave a famous speech at a strategic time about four freedoms that the people and governments of the world should endeavor to respect and protect for all. Roosevelt's four freedoms were Freedom of *speech*, Freedom of *religion*, Freedom from *want*, and Freedom from *fear*. It's a great list, but I suggest that the Prophet Micah gave us another, similar list of four freedoms in Micah 4:1-5.

- Freedom from *ignorance* (**He will teach us His ways**).
- Freedom from *war* (**Neither shall they learn war anymore**).
- Freedom from *want* (**everyone shall sit under his vine and under his fig tree**).
- Freedom from *fear* (**no one shall make them afraid**).

First, "**He will teach us His ways**." With the prophet's eye Micah saw the world streaming into Jerusalem to meet with the Lord God, and to know Him better. It was a time when the world would truly take advantage of the wonderful offer of real relationship with God and know Him and **His ways**.

Second, "**Nation shall not lift up sword against nation, neither shall they learn war anymore**." It is important to see that this is not the peace of capitulation. This is the peace of enforced righteousness. There is no more war, and no more need for **swords** - so why not make them into **plowshares**? There is no more war because there is a new ruler on earth, Jesus Christ. The reigning Messiah will settle all disputes, and "**He shall judge between many peoples**." Conflicts between nations and individuals will be justly and decisively resolved by the Messiah and those who reign with Him ("**He shall judge between the nations, and shall rebuke many people**").

Third, "**Everyone shall sit under his vine and under his fig tree**." This is a proverbial expression that means prosperity and peace. Under the reign of the Messiah, the world will produce as it should have at the beginning – and the greed and tyranny of man will not be allowed to starve others.

Finally, "**No one shall make them afraid**." This means a true freedom from *fear*. Under the rule of Messiah the King, there is perfect peace and administration of justice on the earth. This fourth freedom grows out of the first three. Where there is freedom from ignorance, war, and want, then there is also true freedom from fear.

These glorious promises will be ultimately fulfilled when Jesus reigns over this earth. But we can enjoy a measure – a substantial measure – of these four freedoms *right now*, by enjoying and accepting and submitting to the reign of Messiah the King. In the presence of the Kingdom of Jesus, these freedoms really are just as close as your own hand (Matthew 4:17).

FORTY
Bible Reading: Micah 5

FROM ETERNITY TO HERE

But you, Bethlehem Ephrathah, though you are little among the thousands of Judah, yet out of you shall come forth to Me the One to be Ruler in Israel, Whose goings forth are from of old, from everlasting. (Micah 5:2)

The verse right before Micah 5:2 was another promise of judgment against Israel – but it seems that God can never announce judgment without giving a hopeful promise. And here, through the Prophet Micah, it promises the ultimate hope: the coming of the Messiah. **"But you, Bethlehem Ephrathah...out of you shall come forth to Me the One to be Ruler in Israel."** In this time of humiliation under foreign powers, God will raise up a great **Ruler** from a humble place – **Bethlehem**, the hometown of David, Israel's greatest king; yet it was never a great or influential city. It was truly **little among the thousands of Israel**. Yet God chose it as the birthplace of the Messiah, the **Ruler in Israel**. This passage pinpoints the birthplace of the Messiah hundreds of years before He was born.

It was right for Jesus to be born in that place, because **Bethlehem** means *House of Bread*, and Jesus is the Bread of Life (John 6:35). The name **Ephrathah** means "fruitfulness" or "abundance." This is where our fruitfulness and abundance comes from; as Charles Spurgeon wrote, "Our poor barren hearts never produced one fruit or flower, till they were watered with the Savior's blood."

The Messiah was going *to* Bethlehem, but He was coming from eternity: **"Whose goings forth are from of old, from everlasting."** This glorious promise was fulfilled in Jesus Christ, and Micah's prophetic voice declares that though Jesus came from Bethlehem, He did not *begin* there. His **goings forth** are from eternity past.

Knowing that Jesus' **goings forth are from of old, from everlasting** shows us some important things:

It shows us the *glory* of Jesus, that He is far more than a man. Many people are willing to count Jesus as a great man, or even as the greatest man. This is not enough.

• He said that He was God; and if *knew* that He was not God, then He was a liar.

• He said that He was God; and if He was not and *did not* know He was not God, then He was a lunatic.

• But if He was who He said He was, then He is Lord of all creation – the one from eternity.

It shows us the *love* of Jesus, that He would leave the glory of heaven for us. It's hard to move from a great place to a lesser place, and no place is greater than heaven. Yet He left the ivory palaces of heaven, leaving that glory out of love for us.

It shows us the *nature* of Jesus, that He would add humanity to His deity. It's wrong to think that Jesus was half man and half God, or that He was God on the inside but man on the outside. Instead, the Biblical way to think about the nature of Jesus was that He was fully God and fully man; that the Second Person of the Trinity *added* humanity to His deity. The incarnation was *addition*, not *subtraction*.

It shows us the *sympathy* of Jesus, that He remains fully man and fully God. 1 Timothy 2:5 reminds us that Jesus is *still* fully man and fully God. He didn't give up His humanity when He ascended to heaven. This means that the Savior born in Bethlehem – just as Micah prophesied – has an enduring sympathy with us.

This blessed place of Bethlehem – little among thousands – was specially chosen to bring forth the greatest gift of all: God becoming man. God can use little place and little people to bring forth great gifts. Receive the gift thankfully.

FORTY-ONE

Bible Reading: Micah 6

HE HAS SHOWN YOU

He has shown you, O man, what is good; and what does the LORD require of you but to do justly, to love mercy, and to walk humbly with your God? (Micah 6:8)

Micah 6 begins with a courtroom scene – the prophet pictures a court of law, with Israel "on trial" before the LORD. In the presence of unshakable witnesses (such as "*the mountains*" and "*the hills*" and the "*strong foundations of the earth*"), the court comes to order. God says to Israel, "*Arise, plead your case*" – and God brought His case, His **complaint** against Israel.

As Israel steps up to the witness stand, God asks them, "*What have I done to you?*" The LORD had done nothing but good to Israel, yet He was repaid with rejection and rebellion. Then He reminded Israel, "*I redeemed you from the house of bondage.*" Not only did God *not* do evil to Israel, He also did them an enormous amount of *good*. He redeemed them and gave them godly leaders. God's case against Israel was very strong.

It was time for Israel to answer these charges from God. From the witness box they protested: "*With what shall I come before the LORD?*" This was a question asked out of bitterness and resentment. Israel called out to God from the witness stand, and said: "Just what do You want from me?" They continued, "*Will the LORD be pleased with thousands of rams, ten thousand rivers of oil?*" We can almost hear Israel shouting at God from the witness stand. "You ask too much, God. Nothing will satisfy You. If we brought thousands of rams or rivers of oil or even my own firstborn it would not be enough. You are unreasonable."

Then comes our verse for consideration, Micah 6:8: **He has shown you, O man, what *is* good; and what does the LORD**

require of you but to do justly, to love mercy, and to walk humbly with your God? With this, God stopped the shouting of the angry defendant from the witness box. "You act as if it is some mystery what I require of you. In point of fact it is no mystery at all. I have **shown you** clearly **what is good** and what I **require of you**."

Simply, it was "**To do justly, to love mercy, and to walk humbly with your God**." The LORD answered the contentious witness in open court. "What I require of you isn't complicated. Simply do three things."

• **Do justly**: "Act in a just, fair way towards others. Treat them the way you want to be treated."

• **Love mercy**: "Don't just show mercy, but *love* to show it. Give others the same measure of mercy you want to receive from Me."

• **Walk humbly with your God**: "Remember who I am - *your God*. If you keep that in mind, you will *walk humbly* before Me."

When God exposed Israel's rebellion and ingratitude in open court, they protested that He asked too much. With the reply of Micah 6:8, God demonstrated that He *does not* ask too much of man. He even broke it down to three things. Therefore, God proved His case before the court. Israel was afflicted, but it was not because God neglected or disregarded them. Their own sin brought their affliction upon them. In addition, what God required of them was not mysterious or too difficult - they simply did not do it.

Do justly, love mercy, and walk humbly with your God. Informed by the word of God, motivated by your relationship with God, and empowered by the Spirit of God, you can do it. It isn't too much for Him to ask.

FORTY-TWO

Bible Reading: Micah 7

WHO IS A GOD LIKE YOU?

Who is a God like You, pardoning iniquity and passing over the transgression of the remnant of His heritage? He does not retain His anger forever, because He delights in mercy. He will again have compassion on us, and will subdue our iniquities. You will cast all our sins into the depths of the sea. You will give truth to Jacob and mercy to Abraham, which You have sworn to our fathers from days of old. (Micah 7:18-20)

The name Micah means, "Who is like the Yahweh?" Now at the end of his prophecy, he asked the question, "**Who is a God like You**"? Like many other books of the Minor Prophets, Micah ends his writings with a glorious hope of restoration – so glorious that it made him reflect on the nature of God and ask this question. Micah glorified the God of such great forgiveness ("**pardoning iniquity and passing over the transgression of the remnant of His heritage**"). Micah saw that God's forgiveness was so great, that it can't even be compared to what often passes for forgiveness among men.

God does it for a simple reason: "**Because He delights in mercy.**" The reasons are in *Him*, not in His people. It is simply "**because He delights in mercy.**" Some people question the mercy of God, so it is best to deal with such questions.

If God **delights in mercy**, *then why are some men lost?* Because God will never promote His mercy in a way that brings shame to His justice. God opens His hand of mercy to all who will receive it, but those who will not receive His mercy can blame only themselves.

If God **delights in mercy**, *then why is He not <u>always</u> merciful?* Because there will come a time when the guilty *must* be punished. God's judgments are in themselves expressions of mercy, because they are like the cutting away of cancer. The surgery hurts, but must take place or the whole body will die.

If God **delights in mercy**, *then why is there an unpardonable sin?* We should be grateful that there is only one unpardonable sin - the sin of rejecting His mercy.

If God **delights in mercy**, *then why do I feel that He can't have mercy on me?* In such cases, we should trust God and take Him at His word instead of trusting our feelings.

Look what God does with this great mercy: "**He will again have compassion on us**." God's people once knew His compassion, but they resisted and rejected it. Now they can know it again, confident that **He will again have compassion on us**. And in His compassion, the LORD "**will subdue our iniquities**." He loves us as sinners, but loves us too much to leave us there. His **compassion** saves us from our sin.

His **compassion** is also shown in that the LORD "**will cast all our sins into the depths of the sea**." God will not hold on to our sin, but He will forgive us instead. This means there is no probation with God's forgiveness. He doesn't forgive our sins just to leave them around to hang over our head. In His **compassion**, He does away with our sins, casting them **to the depths of the sea** - and then He puts a "No Fishing" sign there!

Look at the last line of the Book of Micah: "**Which you have sworn to our fathers from days of old**." In concluding His prophecy, Micah saw God's future work as a continuation of His past work to the **fathers** of Israel. Micah knew that the same love, compassion, and mercy He showed to their **fathers** were also available to them - if they received it in faith. We can enjoy the same mercy, standing in a long continuous line of those saved by faith and forgiven by trusting in God's perfect sacrifice. Everyone can stand in the same line, if they will receive it in faith. Let God show you what a great God He is – and then let Him show someone else what a great God He is *through* you.

FORTY-THREE
Bible Reading: Nahum 1

THE JUDGMENTS OF A MERCIFUL GOD

Who can stand before His indignation? And who can endure the fierceness of His anger? His fury is poured out like fire, and the rocks are thrown down by Him. The LORD is good, a stronghold in the day of trouble; and He knows those who trust in Him. But with an overflowing flood He will make an utter end of its place, and darkness will pursue His enemies. (Nahum 1:6-8)

Nahum is one of the more obscure prophets of the Bible. We don't know exactly when he made this prophecy, or exactly where he was from. But the subject is clear enough. Nahum spoke against the superpower nation of his day – the mighty Assyrian Empire, and most specifically, its capital city of Nineveh. Nahum saw through the power and prestige and looked at their deep-seated sin. With powerful images he warned them of the coming judgment of God, and thereby gave them the opportunity to repent.

"**Who can stand before His indignation?**" Nahum knew that people need to understand that they can't fight against God and hope to prevail. Everyone who sets themselves against God will end up standing before **His indignation**, and no one can "**endure the fierceness of His anger.**"

In fact, "**His fury is poured out like fire.**" When God is resisted long enough and rejected strongly enough, eventually His judgment comes. He is *slow to anger* (as it says in Nahum 1:3), but when it does come **His fury is poured out like fire**. Understanding this should make man quick to repent and wary of presuming on God's patience.

When we do turn to the LORD, we find that the "**LORD is good, a stronghold in the day of trouble.**" Those who love Him and trust Him see the goodness of God, and find protection in His **stronghold** - which is the LORD Himself.

At the end of it all, even with the specter of judgment lurking over a wicked city like Nineveh, Nahum could still see and say that "The LORD is good." This may be the most fundamental thing for every human being to know about God.

- God is **good** in His very being - it is His very *nature* to be good.
- God is **good** independently - no one must *help* Him be good.
- God is **good** eternally and unchangeably.
- God is **good** in each one of His Divine Persons.
- God is **good** in all His acts of grace.
- God is **good** in all His plans and purposes for our life.

Yet His goodness does not cancel out His righteousness; in fact, His goodness *shapes* His righteousness. God is a righteous judge *because* He is good. Therefore, Nahum could say of Nineveh, "**With an overflowing flood He will make an utter end of its place**." Taking into account the character of God, though He is slow to anger and good, He cannot forever overlook the sin and rebellion of the Assyrians. Their end in judgment will come like "**an overflowing flood**."

The **overflowing flood** was fulfilled both figuratively and literally. Nineveh was destroyed so completely that an "**utter end of its place**" was literally made. The people and place of Nineveh were lost to history until the 1840s, when the site was finally discovered by archaeologists.

To reject the goodness of God is to invite the demonstration of His righteousness. Instead, receive His goodness today and thank Him for it.

FORTY-FOUR
Bible Reading: Nahum 2

FOR AND AGAINST

"Behold, I am against you," says the Lord of hosts, "I will burn your chariots in smoke, and the sword shall devour your young lions; I will cut off your prey from the earth, and the voice of your messengers shall be heard no more." (Nahum 2:13)

Ask anyone to name some of the great prophets of the Old Testament and they probably will not mention Nahum. His book is short in length and not primarily addressed to the people of Israel. Instead, the prophet Nahum of Israel spoke against the political and military superpower of his day – the Assyrian Empire. Specifically, this book is a pronouncement of judgment against the city of Nineveh, the capital city of Assyria.

This city heard the preaching of Jonah a hundred years before and repented. But at this later time Nahum addressed a city that had slipped back into sin and was again ripe for judgment. In chapter two – which is really a masterpiece of ancient literature – Nahum spoke in vivid images about the assault of an attacking army against Nineveh. In Nahum 2:13, the last verse of the chapter, God vowed to conquer the stubborn and evil city – and states simply in His vow, **"Behold, I am against you."**

Think of those words: **"Behold, I am against you."** Those are *terrible* words to hear from God! We rightly celebrate the truth of Romans 8:31: *What then shall we say to these things? If God is for us, who can be against us?* This principle is true and at work in the life of the Christian, the one who has put their faith in Jesus and lives by that same faith. If God is for you, then it doesn't matter who is against you. It doesn't matter because one person with God is an unconquerable majority.

Accordingly, the opposite is also true - if God is **against you**, then who can be for you? If you set yourself against God, you can only expect to lose. Your arms are too short to box with God, and that is why it is more important than ever to be a Romans 8:31 person instead of a Nahum 2:13 person – to have God *for* you instead of *against* you.

Certainly some people in this work *think* that God is for them when He is not. Others think that God is *against* them when He is not. How can one know for certain? We simply find someone we *know* is on God's side – Jesus of Nazareth. Then by faith we connect ourselves to Jesus, and do everything we can to stay in that connection and to nurture the strength of it. Of course all the while God is working in us and through us to do these things, but since He works through our will and choices, we need to *decide* to do this.

When we are with Jesus, we can be assured that *God is for us.* Your heart is weak and tends towards legalism and unbelief – yet *God is for* you. You have failed God time and again, but He is *for* you. You are often ignorant; but He is *for* you. You have not yet brought forth much fruit; but He is *for* you. God the Father is undeniably for Jesus; as you are in Jesus, He is also *for* you.

It wasn't that way for the proud city of Nineveh so Nahum could say with authority, "**The voice of your messengers shall be heard no more.**" Nineveh enjoyed its status as a power-center of the world, and relished the fact that the **voice** of her **messengers** commanded attention in palaces all over the world. That day would come to an end under the judgment of God, because He was against them.

Is God for you or against you? The key is your faith-connection with Jesus; connected with a real, living faith that shows itself in action, not merely opinions. Keep the connection and get excited: *God is for you.*

FORTY-FIVE

Bible Reading: Nahum 3

CLAPPING FOR JUDGMENT

Your shepherds slumber, O king of Assyria; your nobles rest in the dust. Your people are scattered on the mountains, and no one gathers them. Your injury has no healing, your wound is severe. All who hear news of you will clap their hands over you, for upon whom has not your wickedness passed continually? (Nahum 3:18-19)

Out from his obscurity, the prophet Nahum speaks to us across the centuries. He made his prophecy against the superpower nation of his day – the mighty Assyrian Empire, and most specifically, its capital city of Nineveh. Nahum saw through the power and prestige and looked at their deep-seated sin. With powerful images he warned them of the coming judgment of God, and thereby gave them the opportunity to repent. He prophesied more than 100 years after Jonah first preached to Nineveh, and there was great repentance and revival in Jonah's time. Those days of spiritual renewal were long forgotten, and Nahum saw the destruction that was certain for the unrepentant city.

The coming judgment would afflict the leaders of the city, including the **shepherds** and the **nobles**. Every class of these leaders were numerous in Nineveh, but they all would be ineffective and come to nothing in the day of judgment. Despite their numbers, still it would one day be said that "**Your people are scattered on the mountains, and no one gathers them**." The sinful and rebellious leadership of Nineveh would prove powerless against the judgment of God.

Since the Assyrian Empire was noted for its brutality and cruelty, no one in their neighbor nations would be sorry to hear the news of their downfall. Nahum predicted this: "**All who hear news of you will clap their hands over you**." Nahum thus ended his prophecy with a view of the righteous and their triumph over the unrighteous.

This is something that the people of God need to be often reminded of, because it often goes against present appearances. In the here and now the wicked often not only seem to triumph, they often seem to enjoy it all along the way.

In Psalm 73, the songwriter Asaph dealt with this same problem. It seemed to him that the wicked constantly prospered and lived at ease. It troubled him so much that he doubted his own walk with God. He then explained what changed for him: "*Until I went into the sanctuary of God; then I understood their end. Surely You set them in slippery places; You cast them down to destruction. Oh, how they are brought to desolation, as in a moment! They are utterly consumed with terrors.*" (Psalm 73:17-19)

It isn't wrong for us to long for a righteous resolution of all things in the here and now, but at the same time we recognize that there are some things that will not be settled until they are set in the balances of eternity. In our individual, personal lives, we don't seek the vengeance that belongs to the LORD – we leave it to Him, confident that He can judge whether it is better to bring the judgment now or later.

For Nahum, for Asaph, and for us today, we take comfort in knowing that the judgments of the LORD are faithful and true. We don't need to envy the unrighteous or seek vengeance against them ourselves. Nahum and Asaph each show us that God is more than able to take care of them and us, each according to His promise.

FORTY-SIX
Bible Reading: Habakkuk 1

ARE WE THERE YET?

O LORD, how long shall I cry, and You will not hear? Even cry out to You, "Violence!" and You will not save. Why do You show me iniquity, and cause me to see trouble? For plundering and violence are before me; there is strife, and contention arises. Therefore the law is powerless, and justice never goes forth. For the wicked surround the righteous; therefore perverse judgment proceeds. (Habakkuk 1:2-4)

Habakkuk prophesied during a time of decline in spiritual life among the people of Judah; sometime before the coming of the mighty Babylonian army and their destruction of Judah. It is likely that Habakkuk lived during the time of godly King Josiah (640 to 609 B.C.) and he gave this prophecy during the reign of one of Josiah's successors. Habakkuk knew what it was like to live during a time of revival, and then to see God's people and the nation slip into lethargy and sin. His problem was simple: having seen the spiritual high of revival, it was hard to accept the low of spiritual decline.

Habakkuk asked God questions about these problems of spiritual decline and coming judgment. In this passage he was like the child riding in the vacation-bound car, who can't keep from asking "Are we there yet?" For Habakkuk, the "there" was the judgment of the wicked. He wanted to know why God hadn't arrived at *that* destination yet. Habakkuk looked at the **violence** and injustice around him in the nation of Judah. He wondered where God was, and why God did not set things right.

Troubled, he asked God: "**Why do You show me iniquity, and cause me to see trouble?**" Why does God allow us to see iniquity and trouble, in our self or in others? I can think of three good reasons why God shows us iniquity in our self: To keep us humble; to keep us submissive to Him in trouble; and to make us value salvation all the more.

I can think of four reasons why God allows us to see iniquity in others: To show us what we might have been ourselves, without God's gracious work in us; to make us see the wickedness of sin, that we might pass by it and hate it, and not indulge in it ourselves; to make us admire the grace of God when He saves sinners; and to set us more earnestly to work that God can use us to save others and extend God's kingdom.

It's good to know when you are discouraged and frustrated because it seems like all you see around you is sin and wickedness. God has a purpose in it all. It isn't an *easy* purpose, and it was hard for Habakkuk to deal with. Look at how powerfully he saw wickedness at work in his vocabulary in these verses. He saw: "**Iniquity... trouble...plundering and violence...strife...contention...the law is powerless...justice never goes forth...perverse judgment proceeds**." Habakkuk saw trouble and sin everywhere, from personal relationships all the way to the courts of law. This distressed him so much that he cried out to God and asked God why He didn't set things straight.

Habakkuk deals with the questions that come up when someone really believes God, yet looks around them and the world doesn't seem to match up with how God wants it. Habakkuk saw it - especially remembering the prior times of revival under King Josiah - and asked, "Lord, why do You allow this?" We might say that his impatience was *created* by his faith. He had these problems because he *did* believe in a good God who loved righteousness.

Habakkuk's question and answer time with God shows us that God cares about these questions deep within us, and He has the answers. If you are troubled by these questions, rest in knowing that God has already dealt with them – and will speak them fresh again to the seeking heart. Your problems in this area may be *created* by your faith; but they are also *solved* by faith. Habakkuk will show you how.

FORTY-SEVEN
Bible Reading: Habakkuk 2

WHAT TO LIVE BY

Behold the proud, his soul is not upright in him; but the just shall live by his faith. (Habakkuk 2:4)

Habakkuk knew that judgment was coming upon Judah, and that God would use the Empire of Babylon to bring it. Knowing this, Habakkuk wondered why Babylon - a nation even more sinful than Judah - would be used to bring judgment to Judah. He saw Babylon as the **proud** nation – proud, yet still used by God to bring judgment to Judah. In answering the prophet, God first assures him that He sees **the proud**, and knows that **his soul is not upright in him**.

Pride is everywhere and takes all manner of shapes.

- The rich man is proud of what he has; the poor man proud of having less.
- The talented man is proud of what he can do; the man of few talents is proud of his hard work.
- The religious man is proud of his religion; the unbeliever is proud of his unbelief.
- The establishment man is proud of his place in society; the counter-cultural man is proud of his outcast status.
- The learned man is proud of his intelligence and learning; the simple man is proud of his simplicity.

Satan can persuade the praying brother to be proud of his ability to pray, the growing brother to be proud of his growth, and even the humble brother to be proud of his humility.

At the same time, there is a wonderful contrast to the proud: **But the just shall live by his faith**. In contrast to **the proud**, there are **the just**. The principle of their life is **faith**, instead of pride that looks to self. True **faith** looks outside of self unto the LORD God, while pride always looks to self.

This brief statement from the prophet Habakkuk is one of the most important, and most quoted Old Testament statements in the New Testament. Paul used it to show that the **just** live **by faith**, not by law. Being under the law isn't the way to be found **just** before God, only living by faith is.

Before his bold declaration of the truth of the gospel, Martin Luther was a monk. He went on a pilgrimage to Rome and as he crossed the Alps he fell deathly ill. He remembered a verse that had previously touched him: *The just will live by his faith*, from Habakkuk 2:4. He went on to Rome and one day he came to a church where there is a staircase said to be from Pilate's judgment hall. It was the custom to climb this staircase painfully a step at a time on the knees, saying prayers and kissing the steps. Luther came to this place and starting doing just as all the other pilgrims. As he did this, Luther remembered the words from Habakkuk: *The just will live by his faith*. It is said that when he remembered this he stopped, stood up, walked down and went straight home to Germany. Some say the Reformation began on those stairs.

We are therefore called to live by faith, and nothing else.

- Some Christians live by devotions.
- Some Christians live by works.
- Some Christians live by feelings.
- Some Christians live by circumstances.

Each of these is meaningless and perhaps *dangerous* without faith. What do you live by?

FORTY-EIGHT

Bible Reading: Habakkuk 3

A PRAYER FOR REVIVAL

A prayer of Habakkuk the prophet, on Shigionoth. O LORD, I have heard your speech and was afraid; O LORD, revive Your work in the midst of the years! In the midst of the years make it known; in wrath remember mercy. (Habakkuk 3:1-2)

This concluding chapter of Habakkuk's brief book signals a different approach. The first two chapters of Habakkuk gave us the prophet's "question and answer" time with God. Now that God answered Habakkuk, the prophet brought a prayer to close the book.

The prayer was simple: **O LORD, revive Your work in the midst of the years**. Habakkuk simply prayed for *revival*. He knew how God once worked and how His people once responded, and Habakkuk wanted to see that again.

This prayer of Habakkuk shows us that revival is a work of God and not the achievement of man. It also shows us that there is something man can and must do for revival - simply cry out to God and plead for His reviving work.

Notice the prayer: **revive Your work**. Often, my prayer is really "revive *my* work," but I must have a heart and mind for God's work, far bigger than my portion of it. Get rid of every bit of self-interest and ambition on behalf of yourself, your church, or your denomination. If God were pleased to wonderfully revive your church, but to *more wonderfully* revive another, you should be well pleased with His wisdom. Lose concern for you own glory and advancement, and ask God to revive *His* work.

At the same time, this must be a *personal* prayer: "Lord, revive *me*." We too often blame others or the church in general for sin, corruption, laziness, prayerlessness, lack of spiritual power, or whatever - and we forget that *we are the church*. It is easy to fall into the prayer of pride and say, "Lord, revive *them*. Bring them up to the spiritual standing that *I* have." Don't let that happen. Real revival has to begin and continue with us as individuals – with *me*.

The prayer of Habakkuk did not end there. He went on to ask, **"In the midst of the years make it known."** Habakkuk longed for God to do a work that was *evident* to everyone as a work of God. Whatever happened, he wanted it clear that it was the LORD's doing and not man's. He prayed that revival would be **known** at a definite *time and place* (**in the midst of the years**), not just as an idea in someone's head.

At the end of his prayer, he added the important request: "**In wrath remember mercy**." Habakkuk prayed knowing well that they didn't *deserve* revival, so he prayed for **mercy**. The idea is, "LORD, I know that we deserve your **wrath**, but in the midst of your **wrath remember mercy** and send revival among us."

When we think of all God has given His people in both spiritual and material resources, we say with sorrow that in general (there are blessed exceptions) the people of God have done so little for Him that we deserve to be banished from Him. Therefore, we pray for revival – but we pray on the ground of **mercy**, not merit.

Charles Spurgeon, the great preacher of Victorian England, summarized the idea beautifully: "O God, have mercy upon thy poor church, and visit her, and revive her. She has but a little strength; she has desired to keep thy word; oh, refresh her; restore to her thy power, and give her yet to be great in this land." Amen.

FORTY-NINE
Bible Reading: Zephaniah 1

THE SEARCHLAMPS OF GOD

And it shall come to pass at that time that I will search Jerusalem with lamps, and punish the men who are settled in complacency, who say in their heart, "The LORD will not do good, nor will He do evil."
(Zephaniah 1:12)

As a prophet, Zephaniah was different from other prophets because he tells us both his time and his roots. Zephaniah was an unusual prophet, in that he was of royal lineage, descending from the godly King Hezekiah. His name meant "Yahweh Hides" or "Yahweh Has Hidden." Zephaniah was almost certainly born during the long, wicked reign of Manasseh, whose reign began 55 years before the start of King Josiah's reign. Zephaniah was probably hidden for his own protection.

It was in those days of King Josiah that Zephaniah served as a prophet. Josiah was a godly, young king who brought great revival and reform to Judah. Yet Josiah's reign began 10 years before he led his great revival. The prophecies of Zephaniah were likely given in the years before the revival, and God used this prophecy to bring and to further that great work of grace.

To prepare the nation for revival, God used a warning of judgment. In this passage from Zephaniah, God warned "**I will search Jerusalem with lamps**." The idea is that God would make a careful search through Jerusalem, and look into every hidden part. That meant that no one would be able to hide against the judgment of God. It was coming, and even if God must get out the flashlights, He would find everything worthy of judgment and correction.

The picture reminds us of the story of the old pre-Christian Greek philosopher named Diogenes. It was said that he wandered the streets of Athens with a lantern, looking into the face of every man he met – searching for an *honest* man. Yet when Zephaniah tells us that God uses **lamps** to search out Jerusalem, He isn't doing it to find an honest man – but to uncover sin. It reminds us that we can't hide anything from God. He shines His discerning light upon us and can easily see our hidden sin. Perhaps the people of Jerusalem thought that because their sin was hidden before man that it was also hidden before God. Zephaniah wanted to correct them and us of such a foolish idea.

Once the sin was discovered, God told them what He would do next: "**Punish the men who are settled in complacency.**" The LORD promised judgment against those who felt that God was distant or detached from their lives, and had therefore become complacent.

Then Zephaniah quoted the words of a complacent heart: "**The LORD will not do good, nor will He do evil**." Some people believe that God is detached from this world, and if He is out there He is silent – and therefore irrelevant. Zephaniah wanted to search out this error and correct it – to let everyone know that God *was* active and that they should live in light of it. The bottom line is that both those who believe there is no God and those that believe that if He does exist He has nothing to do with man, are both terribly and tragically wrong.

Edward Gibbon in his book *The Decline and Fall of the Roman Empire* described the attitude towards religion in the last days of the Roman Empire - attitudes remarkably like our own today. He said that the people regarded all religions as equally *true*; the philosophers regarded all religions as equally *false*; and the politicians regarded all religions as equally *useful*. Zephaniah points us to a different idea – that there is a God enthroned in heaven who searches hearts and minds with His shining lamp. Knowing this and acting on the truth of it prepares us for God's work of revival.

FIFTY

Bible Reading: Zephaniah 2

DAYS LIKE CHAFF

*Gather yourselves together, yes, gather together, O undesirable nation,
before the decree is issued, or the day passes like chaff, before the
LORD's fierce anger comes upon you, before the day of the LORD's anger
comes upon you!* (Zephaniah 2:1-2)

The second chapter of Zephaniah is a warning to the nations
to repent and prepare for the coming judgment of God. It is as if
God, in this chapter, gives the nations one last chance to get ready
so they won't be destroyed at His coming. As the chapter develops,
the prophet looked to the west and saw the Philistines – and warned
them. Then he looked to the east and saw the Moabites and the
Ammonites and warned them. Then he looked to the south and saw
the Ethiopians and warned them. Finally, he looked to the north
and warned the Assyrians of the coming judgment of God. Looking
to each point of the compass, the idea was the same: God wanted
everyone to be prepared for His coming. He didn't want *anyone* to
be caught surprised in the day of His judgment.

But, as 1 Peter 4:17 says, judgment begins at the house of God.
If the nations at every point of the compass should prepare for the
coming of God, all the more should Judah and Jerusalem and the
people of God be ready. That's why Zephaniah began the chapter
by speaking to the **undesirable nation** – to the stubborn, unturned
people of God.

First he told them, "**Gather yourselves together**." The idea
was that they should gather together in a solemn demonstration
of national mourning and repentance. An example of this kind of
gathering is found in 1 Samuel 7:5-6, where the prophet Samuel
gathered the people at Mizpah. They mourned over their sin and
repented, and God did great things among them again.

Zephaniah gave them a *time* to gather. They were to do it "**Before the decree is issued**." Here the prophet pled with the nation to repent **before** it was too late.

Then Zephaniah used a beautiful phrase to add a sense of urgency. He warned Israel to get right with God "**Before the day passes like chaff**." Here the prophet called for a sense of *urgency* in repentance. Each day **passes like chaff**, and there is nothing to show for the day if we neglect what is most important: getting right and staying right with God.

Chaff is the thin, light outer husk surrounding a grain of wheat. A handful of chaff had almost no substance and could be carried away with the slightest breeze. How easy it is to let the days pass **like chaff**, and never get right with God! We can allow day after day to pass, lacking any urgency to do what we should before our Creator. We agree that the needs are important, but unconsciously assume that there is plenty of time to address them.

Some people think that the devil's most powerful lie is that there is no God; some people think that the devil's most powerful lie is that there is no truth; some people think that the devil's most powerful lie is that the Bible is not the word of God. But probably the most dangerous lie of the devil is that *there is no hurry*. This is why God speaks to us in several places to have a sense of urgency in getting right with Him. If we don't make it urgent, it may never happen. We can put the emphasis on *now*, "**Before the day passes like chaff**." God wants the separation between you and He to be gone *now*. He doesn't want you to continue in your destructive path another moment. He wants the best for you *now*.

Don't let the days pass like chaff – as if they were light and worthless. The day is heavy with meaning, and today is the day – now is the time.

FIFTY-ONE
Bible Reading: Zephaniah 3

WHEN GOD SINGS

In that day it shall be said to Jerusalem: "Do not fear; Zion, let not your hands be weak. The LORD your God in your midst, the Mighty One, will save; He will rejoice over you with gladness, He will quiet you with His love, He will rejoice over you with singing."
(Zephaniah 3:16-17)

The Book of Zephaniah is one of the more obscure and unknown books of the Bible. Most of it is full of dark prophecies of judgment. It was a book written at the close of almost two generations of godlessness, but at the end of it there is this shining star in the book of Zephaniah - a gem that looks all the more brilliant because it is laid against the black cloth of the judgments of God. These two verses from the third chapter of Zephaniah give something to really remember the book of Zephaniah by. In these verses, Zephaniah gives us five reasons for confidence.

First, be confident because *the LORD is in your midst and He has the power to save*. Remember who it is that stands among you: The LORD your God. The God of all power and glory, not some grandfatherly guy in a rocking chair. No matter what you don't have, take a look at what you do have – you do have the LORD your God in your midst. He is in **your** midst. It's easy to think that He is close to everyone else here, or perhaps this group as a whole, but for some reason He is far away from you. It isn't true - He is in your midst. Draw near to Him and He will draw near to you.

Second, be confident because *God rejoices over you*. Some people think God is like some immensely rich guy who walks the mansions of heaven, bored by everything. That couldn't be further from the truth - God gets excited - He gets excited over us. God knows all about us and His heart is glad. As many faults, as many weaknesses, as many difficulties - He knows them all and still rejoices

Third, be confident because *God gives you rest in His love*. At the beginning of the prophecy of Zephaniah, the LORD told the leaders of Judah to be quiet - but it was more of the "shut your mouth" kind of being quiet. Now God tells His people "I'm going to quiet you with My love." That is a much better way to be quieted.

Fourth, be confident because *God sings over you*. We don't often think of God singing, but He does - He sings **over** His people. God is so happy in His love to his people that He breaks the eternal silence and sun and moon and stars with astonishment hear God chanting a hymn of joy. You should listen to His song and respond to it. Everywhere you go today you see people with ear buds or headphones on and they listen to their own music on their personal audio players. I think that illustrates the way many people listen to their *own* song instead of taking the time and the quiet it takes to listen to God sing over you.

Knowing this is the tender love and care of God for us should make us respond two ways. First, we "**do not fear**" - if the Mighty One loves us and delights in us this way, what can we be afraid of? Refuse to fear. Choke out unbelief. If God rests in His love over you and if He sings over you, what can possibly threaten us? Instead, we trust every loving purpose God has for us. We rest in what Jesus did for us on the cross.

Second, "**let not your hands be weak**." Knowing this mighty Lord of Love is for us, we want to be for *Him* with all of our energy. We will not become weak or weary in our service for Him. The work is not done to earn God's song - that is freely given. But the song inspires us to work.

Take the time and the quiet to listen to His song over you – and let it inspire you to put away fear and to be strong and busy for Him.

FIFTY-TWO
Bible Reading: Haggai 1

UNSATISFIED

Now therefore, thus says the LORD of hosts: "Consider your ways! You have sown much, and bring in little; you eat, but do not have enough; you drink, but you are not filled with drink; you clothe yourselves, but no one is warm; and he who earns wages, earns wages to put into a bag with holes." (Haggai 1:5-6)

The Book of Haggai is the first of the three Minor Prophets written *after* the exile – after some of the children of Israel returned from Babylon. Of the 12 Minor Prophets, the first 9 spoke *before* Judah was carried away captive, exiled to Babylon. Haggai, Zechariah, and Malachi each spoke to those who returned from the 70-year time of exile.

Haggai gave this first word in September, 520 B.C. At that time the exiles had been back in Jerusalem for 18 years - but the work of rebuilding the temple was idle for the previous 14 years. The work started gloriously, according to Ezra 3:10-11. Despite the good beginning, after two years the work stopped, stuck in discouragement and derailed by a lack of focus. When Haggai prophesied the foundation to the temple was laid and the altar of sacrifice was in service, but the temple itself wasn't yet rebuilt. Haggai is mainly a book about *proper priorities*, and how the returning people of Israel had to look past their own comfort and blessing and have a greater concern for the things of God.

We should remember that these weren't "bad people" - they were the remnant that returned from Babylon. Hundreds of thousands of people went into the Babylonian captivity and only about 50,000 returned. Those who did were the most committed to the LORD and to the restoration of Jerusalem. Yet the words of the prophet applied to them: "**Consider your ways!**" The Hebrew figure of speech for this phrase is literally "Put your heart on your roads." Haggai asked

God's people to consider what direction their life was headed, and if they really wanted it to continue that way.

They already suffered from their bad direction: "**You have sown much, and bring in little**." The cause of their financial difficulties was their wrong priorities. They suffered setback after setback because the blessing of God wasn't on their pocketbook. So Haggai described a double curse. Instead of much, little was reaped; and the little that was brought home melted away without doing any good ("**earns wages to put into a bag with holes**"). Despite their feverish activity, little lasting good came of it. It seemed like the faster they went, the more behind they became.

The people of Israel were being judged and they didn't even know it - they probably wrote it all off as bad luck or tough economic times, but God was trying to tell them something. Sometimes our priorities are out of order and we seem to suffer no financial hardship. In such times we should never presume on the mercy of God - we should turn to Him and re-order our priorities before He needs to use crisis to get through to us.

But God wanted to use the present crisis among the returning remnant to get their attention. "**You drink, but you are not filled with drink**." If our priorities are wrong, nothing will satisfy us. Each accomplishment soon reveals that there must be something more, something that can really satisfy.

There is an important word to us today, the voice of the prophet speaking across the centuries. We must take careful account of our life-priorities, and make sure that the things that are important to God are important to us. This conflict between God's priorities and Israel's priorities made an empty life for those who first heard Haggai; if we allow the same conflict we will suffer the same emptiness. Spend some time taking account of your life priorities.

FIFTY-THREE
Bible Reading: Haggai 2

THE DESIRE OF ALL NATIONS

"And I will shake all nations, and they shall come to the Desire of All Nations, and I will fill this temple with glory," says the LORD of hosts. "The silver is Mine, and the gold is Mine," says the LORD of hosts.
(Haggai 2:7-8)

The Book of Haggai brings us into a different period of Biblical history – it spoke to the people of Israel *after* the 70-year Babylonian captivity. The former exiles and their descendents started to trickle back to Jerusalem, and they had a difficult job in front of them. First they had to rebuild the temple, and it was a job filled with discouragement.

The first temple was built at the height of Israel's glory under Solomon. No expense or trouble was spared in making a magnificent temple. Yet these returning exiles were acutely aware that they built their temple with limited resources, both of money and labor. They had a huge, discouraging job in front of them. That is why God wanted to encourage Israel through the Prophet Haggai. In this text, God assured the discouraged builders of the once-glorious temple that their work would have a unique glory, making it even greater than Solomon's temple. The marble and mortar of this second temple might at first be less than Solomon's, but the greatness of a temple is not measured only in marble and mortar.

This second temple would be greater than the first because in it, "**They shall come to the Desire of All Nations**." Through the centuries, most see this as a prophecy of the Messiah coming to this temple rebuilt in the days of Haggai and Ezra. This understanding began with the ancient rabbis and continued among Christians, and fits in well with the promise of filling the "**temple with glory**."

Indeed, Jesus never visited the temple of Solomon – but some 400 years after the time of Haggai, Jesus did visit this second temple first started by Ezra. His presence alone gave this second temple a unique glory. This is certainly true because the true **Desire of All Nations** is Jesus, even if the nations themselves do not know it. When the world cries out for a true reformer, for someone to bring real justice, they unknowingly cry out for Jesus.

If the world could gather up all her right desire; if she could consolidate all her wild wishes in one request; if every true humanitarian could take their philosophies and condense their theories and extract true wisdom from it all – it would all come down to this: send us a God made man. In Jesus this is exactly what we have. The nations grope unaware in the dark, but Jesus is truly "**The Desire of All Nations**."

Knowing that Jesus is the **Desire of All Nations** also encourages our missionary work. This is true in two ways. First, we are confident that the nations desire Jesus even when they are not aware of this desire. This sleeping desire among the nations of this earth assures us that there is an audience for the gospel where ever we go. Second, Jesus is the desire of all nations in the respect that *we* desire Him *for* all nations. This desire drives us to continued missionary prayer, support, and labor.

God gave hope to the temple-rebuilders in a second way. He assured them, "**The silver is Mine, and the gold is Mine**." They didn't have much money for the building project, especially compared to Solomon and the first temple. But instead of being discouraged. They had to boldly trust the God who owned every resource, and then give generously.

This was valuable assurance to the rebuilders in the days of Haggai. It is also assurance for us. God will bring glory to our life and our work with the unique presence of Jesus. God, when trusted as a loving Father, will supply us out of His great unseen resources. Thank God for it all today.

FIFTY-FOUR
Bible Reading: Zechariah 1

RETURN TO ME

Therefore say to them, "Thus says the LORD of hosts: 'Return to Me,' says the LORD of hosts, 'and I will return to you,' says the LORD of hosts." (Zechariah 1:3)

Zechariah began his prophecy with a call to repentance, and a call that remembered the poor spiritual heritage of Israel and Judah. The sin of their fathers doomed the nation to exile, and Zechariah warned the people to remember the same could happen to them.

However, we should remember that these weren't "bad people" - they were the remnant that returned from Babylon. Hundreds of thousands of people went into the Babylonian captivity and only about 50,000 returned. Those who did were the most committed to the LORD and to the restoration of Jerusalem. Yet even they, some 18 years after returning to the Promised Land, needed to hear and heed the warning of the LORD.

The bottom line was that adverse circumstances discouraged God's people, and they wondered why God seemed so far away.

- The land was still desolate after 70 years of neglect.
- The work was hard to rebuild and restore.
- They didn't have a lot of money (Haggai 1:6) or manpower.
- They suffered crop failures and drought (Haggai 1:10-11).
- Hostile enemies resisted the work (Ezra 4:1-5).
- They remembered easier times in Babylon.

Each of these circumstances made them feel that God was far away. Therefore God used Zechariah to assure them that He was *not* distant. If they would return to Him, He would return to them, and that is why Zechariah pled on behalf of the LORD: "**Return to Me...and I will return to you.**"

Sometimes we wish God would *make* us return to Him, instead of *wooing* us to return out of our own choice. We wish that we could just sit back passively and let God spiritually grow us without our own choosing or desire. Nevertheless, God wants our freely given love, so He prompts us to choose Him and **return to** Him.

Zechariah's words remind us of James 4:8: *Draw near to God and He will draw near to you.* This is both an invitation and it is a promise. It is an invitation to come near to God – telling you that *He wants you close to Him.* You don't have to persuade a reluctant God to accept you; He wants you to come close to Him. Zechariah and James agreed on this: "**Return to Me...and I will return to you**." "Draw near to God and He will draw near to you." The invitation is open.

But this is more than an invitation; it is also a promise. God promises to meet us running when we return to Him. We are also reminded that if we are far from God, He hasn't distanced Himself from us. We have distanced ourselves from Him.

An elderly couple drove down the road in their car with a front bench seat. As they drove, the wife noticed that in many of the other cars with couples in the front seat, the woman sat close to the man as he drove. She asked her husband, "Why is it that we don't sit that close anymore?" He simply answered, "I never moved."

If we are far from God, He hasn't moved. We need to return to Him.

FIFTY-FIVE
Bible Reading: Zechariah 2

THE APPLE OF HIS EYE

For thus says the LORD of hosts: "He sent Me after glory, to the nations which plunder you; for he who touches you touches the apple of His eye." (Zechariah 2:8)

By now it has become a common phrase in English – to describe something as "the apple of your eye." Most people don't know that it is in fact a Biblical phrase, don't know exactly what it means, and don't know it's precious and comforting context in the Scriptures.

Most people understand the general meaning of the phrase – that it speaks of something that is precious and valuable to a person. We might describe a son or a daughter as "the apple of our eye." This is its general Biblical idea also, and the phrase is used three other times in the Old Testament (Deuteronomy 32:10, Psalm 17:8, and Proverbs 7:2)

The actual idea behind the phrase is that the "**apple**" of the eye is the pupil – the center and most tender part of the eye, jealously protected by every instinct. Our Creator set our eyes in a protected place, because they are both important and vulnerable. The great English preacher Charles Spurgeon explained it like this: "He esteems them as much as men value their eyesight, and is as careful to protect them from injury, as men are to protect the apple of their eye. The pupil of the eye is the tenderest part of the tenderest organ, and very fitly sets forth the inexpressible tenderness of God's love."

So when God calls His people **the apple of His eye**, there are a few important ideas as to why:

- We are precious to God.
- We are easily injured.
- We need special protection.

In the context from Zechariah 2, we see that the phrase comes in the setting of encouragement to the returning exiles from Babylon. The people of God had been relocated out of the Promised Land by force – and now, after 70 years, God allowed them to come back. Only a small percentage of the exiles and their descendents actually came back, and they came back to a discouraging situation. They needed many things, but especially heavy on their mind was their need for *protection*. Here, God promised to protect and to bless these returning exiles. He even goes so far as to promise that He will protect them as a man protects **the apple of His eye**.

In the Book of 2 Samuel we have the story of a man named Uzziah. When King David brought the Ark of the Covenant into the city of Jerusalem, it was being carried on a cart driven by oxen. As it made its way along the path, something made the cart lurch and it looked for a moment as if the Ark of the Covenant would fall off the cart, and perhaps be ruined. Uzziah reached forward with his hand and did something that was strictly forbidden – he touched the Ark of the Covenant, in the instinctive desire to protect it.

The Ark of the Covenant was important to God; yet God regards His people as even more important. As much as we automatically and zealously protect the center of our eye, so God automatically and zealously protects His people.

Let it flash in your mind each time you hear the phrase **the apple of His eye**: God protects His people. They are precious to Him.

FIFTY-SIX
Bible Reading: Zechariah 3

A BRAND PLUCKED FROM THE FIRE

And the LORD said to Satan, "The LORD rebuke you, Satan! The LORD who has chosen Jerusalem rebuke you! Is this not a brand plucked from the fire?" (Zechariah 3:2)

The Book of Zechariah begins with a series of visions given to the prophet, and among that series is a look at the high priest of Zechariah's day - named Joshua - in the courts of heaven accused by Satan. In the vision Zechariah noticed not only the attack, but also the defense - the LORD Himself drove back the attack of Satan with a strong rebuke.

God does allow Satan to attack and harass His people, but He always strictly regulates what Satan is allowed to do. Satan wanted to destroy Simon Peter, sifting him like wheat (Luke 22:31-32) but Jesus prayed for Peter and stood beside him and did not allow Satan to carry out every evil intention he had against Peter. When spiritual enemies attack God's people, the LORD stands beside His child ever ready to defend in the critical moment. We can trust that when the LORD rebukes Satan, he *is* rebuked - and we can find refuge under His protection.

In the midst of this beautiful scene of God defending the believer the LORD makes what seems to be a strange statement in defense of Joshua. The LORD said of the high priest, "**Is this not a brand plucked from the fire?**" Joshua the high priest had a place of high standing - next to the Angel of the LORD and protected against satanic attack. Still, this place of high privilege was not based on Joshua's own goodness or merit; he himself was rescued as a **brand plucked from the fire**. This is even more boldly stated in that Joshua stood **clothed in filthy garments** (Zechariah 3:3). Satan had a lot to accuse Joshua of, but Joshua had an even greater advocate in the Angel of the LORD.

A **brand** is a burning, burnt, or smoldering piece of wood. Think of a campfire with a blackened, charred chunk of wood smoking in the ashes. It isn't worth much at all and will be consumed completely if it isn't **plucked from the fire**. The brand - especially a brand plucked from the fire - may not be worth anything to anyone else, but God loved this 'brand' and saved it.

This wonderful statement - "**Is this not a brand plucked from the fire?**" - has three wonderful applications. First, it is *an exclamation of amazement* - "this believer is only a brand, yet I have saved him from the fire." Second, it is *an expression of confidence* - "this believer, like a brand, used to be in the fire - but I have plucked him out." Third, it is *a taunt from the LORD to the face of Satan* - "this believer whom you wanted to torment and destroy, *this* one is plucked from your fire!"

Charles Spurgeon said it well, imagining what the Lord might say to the devil in such a situation: "You say this man is black - of course he is: I did not think he was anything else. He is a brand plucked out of the fire. I plucked him out of it. He was burning when he was in it: he is black now he is out of it. He was what I knew he would be; he is not what I mean to make him, but he is what I knew he would be. I have chosen him as a brand plucked out of the fire. What can you say to that?"

When John Wesley was only six years old he was trapped in a burning house and was only rescued when one neighbor climbed on another's shoulders and pulled him out of window. A picture of the scene was drawn for Wesley and he kept the drawing until he died, and wrote under it Zechariah 3:2: *Is this not a brand plucked from the burning?* This is what and who we are - mere brands, but wonderfully saved from the destroying fire by a LORD who loves us and plucked us out for a reason. Today, walk worthy of such a great gift.

FIFTY-SEVEN
Bible Reading: Zechariah 4

NOT BY MIGHT

*So he answered and said to me: "This is the word of
the LORD to Zerubbabel: 'Not by might nor by power,
but by My Spirit,' says the LORD of hosts."* (Zechariah 4:6)

The building project - building a new temple some 70 years after
the Babylonians destroyed Solomon's temple - had stalled for years
and years. Zerubbabel was the civic leader of Jerusalem, and had the
responsibility to finish the work of rebuilding the temple, and he
needed encouragement to carry on the work. God's word came to
him simply and powerfully. '**Not by might nor by power, but by My
Spirit**,' was what the LORD had to say. In the vision of Zechariah 3
God spoke to Zerubbabel about the issue of *purity*. But purity alone
is not enough to accomplish the work of God - the work of God
needs *resources*, and not the resources of human **might** or **power**.

The idea behind the word "might" focuses on *collective* strength,
the resources of a group or army. The word "power" focuses on
individual strength. God says, "not by the resources of many or one,
but by My Spirit. It will not be by your cleverness, your ability, or
your physical strength that the temple will be rebuilt, but by the
Spirit of God." The necessary resource for God's work is the Holy
Spirit and God promises Zerubbabel a rich resource in the Spirit of
God to accomplish His work. When we trust in our own resources
- whether they are small or great in the eyes of man - then we don't
enjoy the full supply of the Spirit.

This great statement is connected to an earlier vision in the
chapter - the vision of the olive trees and the lampstands supplied
by oil coming right from the olive trees. We see that God wanted
Zerubbabel to know that the Holy Spirit would continually supply
his need, just as the oil trees in the vision continually supplied oil to

the lamps on the lampstand. God wants His supply and our reliance on the Holy Spirit to be *continual*.

When we think about it, oil is a good representation of the Holy Spirit:

- Oil *lubricates* when used for that purpose - there is little friction and wear among those who are lubricated by the Spirit of God.
- Oil *heals* and was used as a medicinal treatment in Biblical times (Luke 10:34) - the Spirit of God brings healing and restoration.
- Oil *lights* when it is burned in a lamp - where the Spirit of God is there is light.
- Oil *warms* when it is used as fuel for a flame - where the Spirit of God is there is warmth and comfort.
- Oil *invigorates* when used to massage - the Holy Spirit invigorates us for His service.
- Oil *adorns* when applied as a perfume - the Holy Spirit adorns us and makes us more pleasant to be around.
- Oil *polishes* when used to shine metal - the Holy Spirit wipes away our grime and smoothes out our rough edges.

What our work for the LORD needs is the Holy Spirit. The Holy Spirit works with and through human energy and initiative, but it is possible to have all the energy and initiative, but none of the Spirit. Charles Spurgeon explained it this way: "You all get up plans and say, 'Now, if the church were altered a little bit, it would go on better.' You think if there were different ministers, or different church order, or something different, then all would be well. No, dear friends, it is not there the mistake lies, it is that we want more of the Spirit."

Is that what you want more of? Then ask for an outpouring of the Spirit in your life, and determine that it will not be by might, nor by power, but by His Spirit.

FIFTY-EIGHT
Bible Reading: Zechariah 5-6

BRANCH, PRIEST, AND KING

*Then speak to him, saying, "Thus says the Lord of hosts, saying:
'Behold, the Man whose name is the Branch! From His place He
shall branch out, and He shall build the temple of the Lord; Yes, He
shall build the temple of the Lord. He shall bear the glory, and shall
sit and rule on His throne; so He shall be a priest on His throne, and
the counsel of peace shall be between them both.'"*
(Zechariah 6:12-13)

The text before us speaks of Jesus, as a prophecy of the Messiah
– and it speaks to us in many wonderful ways.

First, it is an *invitation*: "**Behold, the Man**." In the ancient
Hebrew text, the prophecy begins with this phrase. These are the very
words that Pontius Pilate used to present the beaten and bloodied
Jesus of Nazareth to the mob in Jerusalem: "Ecce homo!" When
Pilate said it, he invited the mob to look upon the humiliation of
Jesus. When Zechariah said it, he invited us to look upon Jesus in
triumph and to **Behold, the Man**. We need to do both – to **behold**
Jesus in both His agony and His triumph.

Second, it is a *title*: "**Behold, the Man whose name is the
Branch!**" We already saw this **Branch** in Zechariah 3:8, and it is
a familiar title for the Messiah (Isaiah 4:2 and 11:1, Jeremiah 23:5
and 33:15). The **Branch** is associated with fruitfulness and life.
Jesus used the same image when He said that He was the vine and
we are the branches (John 15:5). Zechariah asked us to look at Jesus
and to consider the life-giving power that He imparts to those who
abide in Him. This is all the more remarkable when we consider the
words, "**From His place He shall branch out**." This speaks of the
fruitfulness and outreaching life of the Messiah. Jesus did not come
only to *have* life, but to *impart* life to others. At your invitation, **He
shall branch out** to bring this life to you.

Third, it is a *promise*: "**And He shall build the temple of the LORD**." This promise was connected with the situation of God's people in the days of Zechariah. Zerubbabel was busy building the temple in Jerusalem, and Zechariah promised that the Messiah would also **build the temple of the LORD** - not the same temple Zerubbabel worked on, but the temple of His people (Ephesians 2:19-22, 1 Peter 2:5). The Bible says that both as *individuals* and *collectively* as the people of God we are being built up into a beautiful work of God – His very own temple and dwelling place.

Finally, it is an *unusual announcement*: "**So He shall be a priest on His throne**." Previously in Israel this was an unthinkable concept because priests did not sit on thrones and kings did not serve as priests. Nevertheless, the **BRANCH** is different; He rules as both a King and Priest.

The ideas are easy to understand, but they are applied over an entire lifetime:

- *Behold Jesus* – Look at Him and meditate upon both His suffering and glory.
- *Receive Him as the Branch* – Connect to His life-giving power, and look for spiritual fruit as evidence of the connection.
- *Consider His building work* – Surrender to His work of building you as His temple, both individually and collectively.
- *Understand Jesus is both King and Priest* – Recognize His reign in your life, and come to the Father through Him as your priest.

Let this ancient prophecy of Zechariah be real in your life today.

FIFTY-NINE
Bible Reading: Zechariah 7

FOR ME OR FOR YOU?

Say to all the people of the land, and to the priests: "When you fasted and mourned in the fifth and seventh months during those seventy years, did you really fast for Me; for Me?" (Zechariah 7:5)

God knows who we are - Psalm 103:13-14 says it like this: "As a father pities his children, so the LORD pities those who fear Him. For He knows our frame; He remembers that we are dust." He knows that we need material, tangible things to help convince us of the reality of the spiritual. God cares about how we regard the material world; He wants us to use it for His glory instead of being a slave to material things. One of the ways God helps us put the material world into perspective is by fasting. A time of fasting shows that we put our spiritual needs and concerns above our material needs and concerns. Yet we can twist a good gift like fasting and use it as an occasion for spiritual pride.

That was exactly the problem in Zechariah's day. The priests fasted all right, but they didn't fast for the right reasons. Point blank, God asked them: "**Did you really fast for Me; for Me?**" God's word through Zechariah rebuked the people of God for what their fasting had become - indulgent pity-parties instead of a time to genuinely seek God. As the prophet explained in the next several verses, their lives were not right when they did eat and drink - that they did for themselves, not for the LORD. A few days of fasting every year could not make up for the rest of the year lived for self.

Isn't it challenging to think about how much we do for our self and not for the LORD? What might the LORD come to us about and say, "Did you really do this for Me, for Me?" When we think about it, we might find that much of our religious service is really done for self, not for God. We can pray in such a manner so that people will admire our prayer. We can sing songs of worship hoping people will hear our great voice - or worry excessively about them hearing our poor voice. Either way, it's all about self, not God.

The great mistake they made in Zechariah's time was thinking that a day of ritualistic fasting could make up for an everyday walk that ignored God. Later, the prophet asked, "Should you not have obeyed the words which the LORD proclaimed?" Because their hearts were not right with God, their rituals were not right before God. Everyday obedience would make their times of fasting meaningful, but their neglect of everyday obedience made their fasting hypocritical.

The point is clear. Both the LORD God and His prophet Zechariah were not against fasting, they were against the *wrong kind* of fasting - fasting that was just a ritual, fasting that thought it could make up for a life in general that ignored God. Used the right way, fasting is a wonderful part of our walk with God - just make sure you do it for the LORD, and not for self.

SIXTY
Bible Reading: Zechariah 8

HOW MARVELOUS

Thus says the LORD of hosts: "If it is marvelous in the eyes of the remnant of this people in these days, will it also be marvelous in My eyes?" Says the LORD of hosts. (Zechariah 8:6)

The eighth chapter of Zechariah is filled with wonderful and amazing prophecies. At the time Zechariah wrote, only a few exiles from Babylon had come back to the Promised Land. Jerusalem was a small city still in many ways a ruin. It was not like its glorious past, there was lots of work to be done, the circumstances were dangerous, and there were not many resources (either financial or human) to do the work. Nevertheless, Zechariah 8 makes some bold promises:

- God is greatly passionate for Jerusalem (Zechariah 8:2).
- God will transform Jerusalem by His own presence (Zechariah 8:3).
- Jerusalem will be called "The City of Truth" and "The Holy Mountain" (Zechariah 8:3).
- Jerusalem will once again be a prosperous, busy, and safe place (Zechariah 8:4-5).

When the people of Zechariah's day looked at the ruins and the state of weakness in the city around them and then heard these wonderful promises, they had a problem. The promises seemed too good to be true; too big, too wonderful, too marvelous. That is what God deals with in Zechariah 8:6 when He asked, **"If it is marvelous in the eyes of the remnant of this people in these days, will it also be marvelous in My eyes?"** The promise of a transformed, prosperous, safe Jerusalem seemed a little too fantastic to believe when the city was half-built and the walls wouldn't be completed for another 60 years.

Yet God wanted them to think, **"Will it also be marvelous in My eyes?"** Just because it seemed too big in the eyes of man, it was not too **marvelous** for the LORD. The people of ancient Jerusalem needed to do what we need to do today: remember how big God is, and that even though something is impossible with man, it isn't that way with God.

Jesus reminded us of the same principle in Mathew 19:26. He said, *"With men this is impossible, but with God all things are possible."* We easily think that God is just a super-man, and forget that He is God and not man. There is more than a Grand Canyon's difference between deity and humanity. It is true that deity and humanity are *compatible*, because God the Son, the Second Member of the Trinity, added humanity to His deity and came to this earth as Jesus Christ. Our compatibility with God is based on the fact that we are made in His image. At the same time, we are still human and He is still divine. We should never assume that if something is too **marvelous** for us, it is too **marvelous** for Him.

The great English preacher Charles Spurgeon preached a memorable sermon on this text, and in it told a story from his boyhood. He remembered that when he was little, he was taken to see the house of a nobleman in England, and a friend went with him. When they entered the house, Spurgeon was absolutely astonished at the largeness of the house. It seemed to him like he had never seen something so big and wonderful. He said aloud, "What a house for a man to live in!"

His friend said, "Bless you, boy; this is only the kitchen!" The young boy Spurgeon had been led in through the kitchen and the servants' quarters, and he was nevertheless astonished at how marvelous it all was – and *he had not even yet seen the mansion*, which of course was a far more wonderful house.

Just because it is too **marvelous** for us doesn't mean it is too **marvelous** for our God.

SIXTY-ONE
Bible Reading: Zechariah 9

THE COMING KING

"Rejoice greatly, O daughter of Zion! Shout, O daughter of Jerusalem! Behold, your King is coming to you; He is just and having salvation, lowly and riding on a donkey, a colt, the foal of a donkey."
(Zechariah 9:9)

Jesus came to a Messiah-expecting world. It is significant to notice the high level of messianic hope in the world of the first century. Yet many or most missed the Messiah when He came, including many of those who earnestly expected Him. This strange and sad situation happened because people looked for the wrong kind of Messiah. They looked for a political power Messiah, not for a humble and lowly savior from sin. This passage from Zechariah reminds us of the kind of Messiah Jesus is, and warns us against hoping or looking for the wrong kind of Savior.

The verse begins, **"Behold your King is coming to you... lowly and riding on a donkey."** This Messiah-King is **lowly**, and in part this was indicated by the animal He rides. He doesn't ride the triumphant stallion of a conquering general, but the customary mount for royalty, coming in peace. This was quite a contrast to the conqueror Alexander the Great, and it challenges us to take the lowly place instead of the place of self-exaltation.

It's easy to recognize pride – *in others*. It can be very hard to recognize it in myself. We can even begin to take a perverse pride in our own humility. We boast that we hate boasting. We flatter ourselves that we hate flattery. When someone tells us that we are really humble, we feel as proud as Lucifer himself may have felt. We think of ourselves as so wise, so experienced, so mature, so discerning, and so free from self-confidence that we are the first to be caught in the trap of self-satisfaction. It is actually a wonderfully deep work of God to make us genuinely humble.

Look back at how the prophet Zechariah described the animal Jesus would ride upon: "**A donkey, a colt, the foal of a donkey**." Taken together, these words seem to form a Hebrew expression of speech emphasizing that the animal is purebred - a truly magnificent, royal mount. He didn't need to ride a horse; this worked against the spirit of Deuteronomy 17:16. Jesus came to fulfill the law, not to abolish it. So He did not come upon a majestic horse, but instead upon a humble – yet fine – donkey.

More importantly, look at how the Messiah would be revealed at his arrival: "**Rejoice greatly...Shout...Behold, your King is coming**." This clearly prophesies what is known as the triumphal entry of Jesus (Matthew 21:5), when He presented Himself as the Messiah to Jerusalem and the people of Israel. It was a joyous occasion, so happy that Jesus said that if the people did not cry out in praise, then the rocks themselves would be forced to worship their Creator.

Though the triumphal entry was a joyful celebration, a Roman spectator would wonder what was so "triumphal" about this entry. It didn't compare at all to the kind of parade Julius Caesar had when he came back to Rome from Gaul. Then there was a parade that lasted three days as he displayed all the captives and booty he brought back. In contrast to this, the procession of Jesus must have seemed pretty humble, and this showed that Jesus was a different kind of King.

Are you expecting the wrong kind of Messiah? Are you looking for a Savior from a Hollywood image, or from the humble servant nature of Jesus? Put your hope and expectation on the right kind of Messiah, and in Him you will find a Savior.

SIXTY-TWO
Bible Reading: Zechariah 10

THE PERFECT SHEPHERD

"My anger is kindled against the shepherds, and I will punish the goatherds. For the LORD of hosts will visit His flock, the house of Judah, and will make them as His royal horse in the battle. From him comes the cornerstone, from him the tent peg, from him the battle bow, from him every ruler together." (Zechariah 10:3-4)

In His anger against the unfaithful leaders of Judah, God promised to set things right. First He would do it by bringing judgment upon these leaders (who are figuratively called **shepherds** here). Yet this is not only a promise of judgment. It also has a great promise of blessing and restoration: "**Will make them as His royal horse in the battle**." In mercy God will take His people and transform them from a **flock** of sheep into a herd of war horses, ready for **battle**. All of them shall be like mighty men and defeat their enemies.

Then comes a wonderful promise. God says of Judah: "**From him comes the cornerstone, from him the tent peg, from him the battle bow, from him every ruler together**." Though God was displeased with Israel's shepherds, He promised to raise up the perfect shepherd **from** (and *for*) Judah. One day the tribe of Judah would bring forth a perfect leader, described in four different ways.

Jesus is the **cornerstone**. This means that He is the foundation, the measure, and the standard. As it says in Isaiah 28:16: *"Therefore thus says the Lord GOD: 'Behold, I lay in Zion a stone for a foundation, a tried stone, a precious cornerstone, a sure foundation; whoever believes will not act hastily.'"* Since Jesus is our **cornerstone**, we can build our life on Him.

Jesus is the **tent peg**. This means that He holds all things securely together. As it says in Isaiah 22:23-24: *"I will fasten him as a peg in a secure place, and he will become a glorious throne to his father's house.*

They will hang on him all the glory of his father's house, the offspring and the posterity, all vessels of small quantity, from the cups to all the pitchers." Since Jesus is our **tent peg**, we can put our full confidence on Him and never be disappointed – He is strong enough to hold us up.

Jesus is the **battle bow**. This means that He is a strong fighter for good. Revelation 19:15 carries this idea: *"Now out of His mouth goes a sharp sword, that with it He should strike the nations. And He Himself will rule them with a rod of iron. He Himself treads the winepress of the fierceness and wrath of Almighty God."* Since Jesus is our **battle bow**, we don't have to fight the battle alone. He is the protector of our cause, and we look to Him for the victory.

Finally, Jesus is the leader over **every ruler** of His people. This means that He is the ultimate leader, the King of Kings and the Lord of Lords, even as it says in Revelation 19:16: *"And He has on His robe and on His thigh a name written: KING OF KINGS AND LORD OF LORDS."* He has all power, all authority, even over the highest king who ever reigned – therefore we should recognize *His* authority in our life.

Each title belongs to Him, because He is the one who comes from Judah to fulfill these promises. Yet they were not only fulfilled for Judah, but also for us – for all who will enter into a trusting relationship with Jesus. Make that *you* today.

- Today, is Jesus your foundation – your **cornerstone**?
- Today, is Jesus your security – your **tent peg**?
- Today, is Jesus your warrior – your **battle bow**?
- Today, is Jesus your Lord – your master over **every ruler**?

Make it so by faith.

SIXTY-THREE
Bible Reading: Zechariah 11

THE FOOLISH SHEPHERD

And the LORD said to me, "Next, take for yourself the implements of a foolish shepherd. For indeed I will raise up a shepherd in the land who will not care for those who are cut off, nor seek the young, nor heal those that are broken, nor feed those that still stand. But he will eat the flesh of the fat and tear their hooves in pieces."
(Zechariah 11:15-16)

In the previous chapter of Zechariah, he announced the coming of the perfect Shepherd unto the people of God. He looked forward to the arrival of the Messiah, and how He would be the promised Shepherd. But sometimes we know things best in contrast, so in this chapter, Zechariah tells us something about a **foolish shepherd**, both so we can avoid such a one and appreciate the perfect Shepherd all the more.

God spoke to Zechariah, telling him to "**Take for yourself the implements of a foolish shepherd.**" The prophet was supposed to play-act as a **foolish shepherd** who did not care for the sheep the way that a shepherd should. He then shows many of the characteristics of the **foolish shepherd**:

- The foolish shepherd **will not care for those who are cut off** but a wise and godly shepherd will seek the lost.
- The foolish shepherd will not **seek the young** but a wise and godly shepherd knows that **the young** need to come to the LORD as much as older people do.
- The foolish shepherd will not **heal those that are broken** but a wise and godly shepherd looks for broken hearts and lives and mends them with God's love and Word.
- The foolish shepherd will not **feed those that still stand** but a wise and godly shepherd will faithfully feed the sheep.

- The foolish shepherd will **eat the flesh of the fat and tear their hooves in pieces** but a wise and godly shepherd will lay down his life for the sheep (John 10:11).

After telling us about the foolish shepherd, God then spoke through Zechariah and told us where he would come from: "**I will raise up a shepherd in the land**." This means that this shepherd *came from God*. In fact, the foolish shepherd is allowed and appointed by God as judgment because His people forsook the true shepherd. One great fulfillment of this was in Israel's rejection of Jesus. They rejected the Good Shepherd (John 10:1-18) but received another shepherd (John 5:43).

This teaches us a valuable lesson. We often assume that people just need the right kind of leader. Here we see that even the ultimate leader may be rejected and a worthless leader chosen instead. Democracy's value is that it respects man's fallen nature and spreads out power - yet the majority *may be* very wrong and prefer a **foolish shepherd** instead of the Good Shepherd.

The days of Jesus, the **foolish shepherd** embraced by Israel was partially fulfilled in their choice of Barabbas (Matthew 27:20-22). Yet there seems to be a future fulfillment also, when this will be ultimately fulfilled in Israel's embrace of the Antichrist and their covenant with him (Daniel 9:27).

Zechariah's prophecy teaches us something about the great themes of God's plan for the world, both past and future. Nevertheless, there is something for us to learn for today. Are you putting your trust in a foolish shepherd? Look at the characteristics of the foolish shepherd that Zechariah described and use them as measuring lines. Most of all, put your trust in the *Perfect Shepherd* of Zechariah 10 who is the contrast to the foolish shepherd of Zechariah 11.

SIXTY-FOUR
Bible Reading: Zechariah 12

LOOKING, WEEPING, AND LIVING

And I will pour on the house of David and on the inhabitants of Jerusalem the Spirit of grace and supplication; then they will look on Me whom they pierced. Yes, they will mourn for Him as one mourns for his only son, and grieve for Him as one grieves for a firstborn.
(Zechariah 12:10)

Zechariah 12 is all about a great outpouring of the Spirit of God upon His ancient people of Israel. He promises to bless, restore, and strengthen them in the last days. As Zechariah tells us in 12:10, part of this great outpouring of strength and might to defend Jerusalem will be an outpouring of the **Spirit** - but for **grace and supplication**. God will move among Israel and bring to them saving grace and repentant prayer.

Then God makes a remarkable promise: "**Then they will look on Me whom they pierced. Yes, they will mourn for Him as one mourns for his only son**." As Jerusalem is supernaturally defended and the Spirit is poured out on the nation, *they will turn to Jesus*, the **pierced** One. His head was **pierced** with thorns, His hands and feet were **pierced** with nails, and a spear **pierced** His side. Look at the promise word by word.

First, "**they will look**." They will turn away from their trust in the foolish and worthless shepherd, and turn their focus on the Good Shepherd. When we see Jesus crucified - understanding why He went to the cross and what He accomplished there - we are drawn to Him in humble repentance (John 12:32).

Second, they will look on Him "**whom they pierced**." They will realize that **they** did it, and that they bear responsibility – certainly not the sole responsibility, but responsibility nonetheless - for the crucifixion of their Savior.

Third, "**they will mourn**." The Jewish people will turn to Jesus in repentance, mourning their past rejection of Him. The mourning will be deep, as if for an **only son**, the **firstborn**. **Firstborn** was synonymous with the most beloved and with hope for the future. Therefore, it expresses the great depth of the mourning that will mark the fulfillment of this prophecy.

This will fulfill the amazing promise of Romans 11:26 (*And so Israel will be saved*) and many other passages that tell us that before the physical return of Jesus to this earth, the Jewish people - as a whole - will welcome Him as their Lord and Savior. The whole context of Zechariah 12 puts this radical conversion in the setting of miraculous deliverance from an attack by the nations.

Yet the prophecy speaks to us today. Look at the order: "**They will look...they will mourn**." Here we see the pattern for coming to Jesus and true repentance. *First* we look to Jesus, and *then* we mourn for our sins. *Looking to Jesus must come first.*

This is a great mistake that is commonly made. It is often believed that we must first mourn over our sins, and then look by faith to Jesus. It is common today for evangelists to think they must make people mourn over their sin *first*, and only after that point them to Jesus Christ. Do we not find a pattern here for something different? Our text gives us a pattern of *first* looking to Jesus, and *then* mourning for our sin. We can tell people to look to Jesus *immediately*.

An old preacher once said something very beautiful: That we are given two eyes, one to look with and the other to weep with. We should do both – look to Jesus, and weep over our own sin. All in all, Zechariah 12 gives us a beautiful picture: the Father sending the Spirit so that men would look upon the Son. Look upon the Son today and live.

SIXTY-FIVE
Bible Reading: Zechariah 13

THERE IS A FOUNTAIN

In that day a fountain shall be opened for the house of David and for the inhabitants of Jerusalem, for sin and for uncleanness.
(Zechariah 13:1)

Zechariah 13 begins with the words, "**In that day**," connecting it with the idea at the end of chapter 12. That chapter ended with Israel's return to the LORD through the once rejected but now embraced Messiah. Flowing from their embrace of the Messiah, they now enjoy **a fountain** that brings cleansing **for sin and for uncleanness**. The cleansing comes after their mourning for the One whom they have pierced.

It is a beautiful promise – this fountain "**shall be opened**." This means that the fountain shall be not simply opened, but it shall remain open. The way to cleansing from the sin, shame, and guilt of our life is always open if we take it by faith.

The picture is all the more wonderful if we remember the geography of ancient Israel – it is pretty much a dry and barren place, without large and lush rivers. The idea of an abundant **fountain** was a glorious and refreshing thought to any of Zechariah's original readers. After all, a fountain is better than a river or a well or a reservoir – the **fountain** brings the water to you! It is a familiar Old Testament idea expressed perhaps most beautifully here in Zechariah.

The idea of the sin-cleansing fountain has also been a part of famous hymns:

There is a fountain filled with blood,
Drawn from Immanuel's veins;
And sinners, plunged beneath that flood,
Lose all their guilty stains.
(William Cowper)

Foul, I to the Fountain fly;
Wash me, Saviour, or I die.
Rock of Ages, cleft for me,
Let me hide myself in thee.
(Augustus Toplady)

The powerful idea in our verse is that the flow of this sin-cleansing **fountain** is *inexhaustible*. After all, this is a *fountain* opened; not a cistern nor a reservoir, but a fountain. This fountain continues still to bubble up, and it is as full after a thousand years as it was at the first. Just so, the provision of God for the forgiveness and the cleansing of our souls continually flows and overflows.

We also notice that it is a fountain **opened**. This tells us that the way for sin and sinfulness to be cleansed is accessible – right now – to all people. No one is excluded, because the fountain is **opened**. It isn't hid and concealed, it isn't closed and barred, but it is a fountain **opened**.

Just what does this open fountain cleanse? Zechariah tells us that it is "**For sin and for uncleanness**." The only thing that can cleanse **sin and uncleanness** is God's **fountain**. It deals both with the sin and with the stain it leaves behind (**uncleanness**). It is of God, and nothing else can cleanse. Our own effort at reform or restitution can't cleanse us; our past, present, or promised works can't cleanse - only His **fountain**.

Let that fountain flow in your life today.

SIXTY-SIX
Bible Reading: Zechariah 14

WHAT A DAY THAT WILL BE

In that day "HOLINESS TO THE LORD" shall be engraved on the bells of the horses. The pots in the LORD's house shall be like the bowls before the altar. Yes, every pot in Jerusalem and Judah shall be holiness to the LORD of hosts. Everyone who sacrifices shall come and take them and cook in them. In that day there shall no longer be a Canaanite in the house of the LORD of hosts. (Zechariah 14:20-21)

The last chapter of Zechariah is like the end of many of the books of the Minor Prophets – filled with hope and the promise of a glorious restoration. Zechariah ends with a look ahead to the time when the glory of the LORD fills the earth, and the rule of the Messiah is enjoyed globally.

In trying to describe the glory of that day, Zechariah tells us "**In that day "HOLINESS TO THE LORD" shall be engraved on the bells of the horses**." That phrase was the great inscription on the metal band around the high priest's headpiece (Exodus 28:36). It was such a sacred phrase that it was reserved for the holy garments of the highest priest of the land of Israel. Yet Zechariah looked forward to a time when this phrase would not be reserved for one golden band on the high priest's headpiece. There will come a day when "**HOLINESS TO THE LORD**" goes on the bells of the horses. After all, in the glory of the Messiah's kingdom horses won't be needed for war any longer - now even they can wear the emblems of **HOLINESS TO THE LORD**.

In telling us about this millennial glory, Zechariah mentions "**The pots in the LORD's house**." In ancient Israel, these were the cooking utensils used to cook the sacrificial meat from the peace offerings. The **bowls before the altar** were used to gather and sprinkle sacrificial blood on the altar. These show that animal sacrifice will continue in the millennium, but *not as atonement for sin* - which was perfectly satisfied by the atoning work of Jesus. Sacrifice in the millennium will look back to the perfect work of Jesus.

But the real point is plain: "**Every pot in Jerusalem and Judah shall be holiness to the LORD of hosts**." In the glory of the Messiah's kingdom, what was previously common is made holy – and the holy is made holier – and the irreclaimably profane is forever shut out. At the end of it all, there is no longer any distinction between the holy and profane. All is set apart to God and His purposes.

The power of this promise is beautiful. God promises that there will come a day when the people and the city will be so holy that even insignificant things like the bells of horses and the pots in the houses will be fully dedicated as holy to the LORD. This is how God wants it in our life today. Everything should be gloriously dedicated to Him, from the pots that you cook with, to the horn of your automobile. It should all belong to Him to bring Him glory.

The Bible often points to a line between the holy and the profane. Some people and things are set apart unto God, and some things are not. What is in God's sphere is holy, and what is out of that sphere is profane. One of the great themes in the Bible is the eventual elimination of this line between the holy and the profane. But there is a right way and a wrong way to eliminate the line between the holy and the profane: you can make everything *holy* (set apart to the LORD), or you can make everything *profane* (set apart to sin and self). Zechariah ends his prophecy making it clear that God's way is to make everything that was once common or profane *holy* instead.

What do you need to write, "**HOLINESS TO THE LORD**" on in your life today?

SIXTY-SEVEN
Bible Reading: Malachi 1

BEING CHOSEN AND CHOOSING

"Yet you say, 'In what way have You loved us?' Was not Esau Jacob's brother?" Says the LORD. "Yet Jacob I have loved; but Esau I have hated, and laid waste his mountains and his heritage for the jackals of the wilderness." (Malachi 1:2-3)

The prophecy of Malachi is built around seven questions the people asked God. These questions revealed their doubting, discouraged, sinful hearts.

- *In what way have You loved us?* (Malachi 1:2)
- *In what way have we despised Your name?* (Malachi 1:6)
- *In what way have we defiled You?* (Malachi 1:7)
- *In what way have we wearied Him?* (Malachi 2:17)
- *In what way shall we return?* (Malachi 3:7)
- *In what way have we robbed You?* (Malachi 3:8)
- *In what way have we spoken against You?* (Malachi 3:13)

The book begins with the kind of question that is rarely spoken, but often harbored in the heart. Israel asked God, "**In what way have You loved us?**" It was as if they asked, "God, if you really love me why are things the way they are?" In answering the question, God directed Israel to His power and authority to choose: "**Yet Jacob I have loved; but Esau I have hated**." God asked Israel to find assurance in His election. He wanted them to understand that they are chosen and remain His chosen and favored people. When the people of Israel compared themselves to their neighbors the Edomites (the descendants of **Esau**), they saw that God chose to preserve Israel and chose to punish the Edomites.

Understanding that God has chosen us can bring a wonderful assurance of God's love. It means that God chose us before we existed and that the reasons for His choosing and loving us are based in

Him, not in us. Knowing God chose us gives us a sense of boldness and confidence in our walk with Him.

We should remember the reason why election is brought up here: not to exclude, but to comfort and reassure. Our greatest error in considering God's election is to think that God chooses for careless reasons, as if He made choices by flipping a coin or pulling petals off of flowers. We may not understand God's reasons for choosing and they may be reasons He alone knows and answers to, but God's choices are not careless. They make perfect sense knowing everything God knows and seeing everything God sees.

Yet this is a text that troubles many. When God said, "**Jacob I have loved; but Esau I have hated**" some wonder how God could *hate* Esau. But it is important to see that He didn't hate Esau in the sense of cursing him or striking out against him. Indeed, Esau was a blessed man (Genesis 33:9, 36:1-43). Yet when God *chose* Jacob, He left Esau *unchosen* in regard to receiving and passing down the blessing first given to Abraham.

Sometimes people wonder, "Am I chosen or not?" This line of thinking may lead some to be fatalistic, and to just figure that God has it all arranged ahead of time, so our reaction or response to Him is futile. We can imagine someone saying, "I don't believe in Jesus; therefore I must not be chosen." That is fine, but then that person cannot blame God at all for not choosing them if they also refuse to choose Him.

It sounds strange, but we can choose Him and discover that we are chosen – and then find comfort in His strong, electing love.

SIXTY-EIGHT
Bible Reading: Malachi 2

SEEING IT LIKE HE DOES

Judah has dealt treacherously, and an abomination has been committed in Israel and in Jerusalem, for Judah has profaned the LORD's holy institution which He loves: he has married the daughter of a foreign god. May the LORD cut off from the tents of Jacob the man who does this, being awake and aware, yet who brings an offering to the LORD of hosts! (Malachi 2:11-12)

Malachi was a prophet very interested in marriage. Here, he speaks for God as he called marriage "**The LORD's holy institution which He loves**." This tells us exactly how God feels about marriage. It is **holy** to Him; it is an **institution** to Him; and God **loves** marriage. Therefore, when we sin against our marriage or our marriage vows, we sin against something **holy** to God. He has *set apart* marriage for a special meaning, a special purpose in the life of His people.

Therefore, when we sin against our marriage or our marriage vows, we sin against an **institution** that God has established. Marriage is God's idea, not man's; He formed and established the first marriage as a pattern for every one afterwards (Genesis 2:20-25). Because it is an **institution**, we are not allowed to define marriage any way that pleases us; God has established it and we must conform to what He has established.

Therefore, when we sin against our marriage or our marriage vows, we sin against something that God **loves**. He **loves** marriage for what it displays about His relationship with us; for the good it does in society; and for the way it meets the needs of men, women, and children. Most of all, God **loves** marriage as a tool for conforming us into the image of His Son.

But the people of Israel in the days of Malachi did not have the same love for the institution of marriage that God did. Instead, they first ignored God's command about *who* to marry: "**He has married the daughter of a foreign god.**" The first *treachery* and **abomination** God addressed was the intermarriage between the people of God and their ungodly neighbors. The dangers of an ungodly intermarriage are well documented in the Old and New Testaments.

God's command against mixed marriages in Israel had nothing to do with race, but with faith. There is even a foreign wife in the genealogy of Jesus - Ruth was a Moabite who married a Jewish man named Boaz; but she forsook Moab's gods for the LORD (Ruth 1:16).

The Book of Malachi goes on to describe a second way that the leaders of Israel sinned against marriage: they had a low regard of the bond of marriage, and saw breaking a marriage as a light thing. Malachi spoke to those who did not take their marriage vows seriously, and considered it a small matter to break up one marriage and to start another. The voice of the prophet needs to be heard today, especially among those who consider themselves as leaders among God's people. That was Malachi's original audience – he spoke to the priests and leaders of Israel in his day.

For some reason, they thought they could sin against marriage in these ways and it would not substantially affect their service of God. Therefore, Malachi warned: "**May the LORD cut off from the tents of Jacob the man who does this, being awake and aware, yet who brings an offering.**" In this, God promised to punish the priests who married foreign, pagan wives and thought that it would not affect their service of the LORD.

Our prayer should be simple: "Lord, give me the same regard for marriage that You have. I want to see it like You do."

SIXTY-NINE
Bible Reading: Malachi 3

REFINER'S FIRE

"But who can endure the day of His coming? And who can stand when He appears? For He is like a refiner's fire and like launderer's soap. He will sit as a refiner and a purifier of silver; He will purify the sons of Levi, and purge them as gold and silver, that they may offer to the LORD an offering in righteousness." (Malachi 3:2-3)

As a prophet, Malachi looked ahead to the coming of the Messiah. In the first verse of chapter 3, he spoke of two messengers to come - one to prepare the way of the LORD, and one to be the *Messenger of the covenant*. Like many Old Testament announcements of the coming of the Messiah, it mingles aspects of His first and His second coming. Therefore, he asked: **"Who can endure the day of His coming?"** He knew that this coming of the Messiah would not be all softness and comfort.

Instead, **"He is like a refiner's fire and like launderer's soap."** The coming of this second Messenger will be awesome and terrible, but with a purpose. Both the launderer and the refiner work to clean, and not to destroy.

He gets more specific: **"He will sit as a refiner and a purifier of silver."** Malachi has in mind a man refining metal, looking into an open furnace or a pot. As the refiner looks into the pot with molten silver, he knows that the process of purifying is complete and all the impurities are burnt away when he can see his own image plainly reflected in the liquid silver.

When you seek the Lord, understand that it means that you are actually seeking a fire to test you, and one that will burn away some things that have been dear to you. We do not expect Jesus to come and save us in our sins, but to save us from our sins; therefore, when we take Jesus as our Savior, we also take Him as our purifier. He might just have to turn the heat up a bit to purify us.

It is wonderful to notice who has the job of refining us: "**He will sit as a refiner**." God will not give this work to anyone else. He may use angels to rescue us when we are in danger, but He would never give the job of purifying us to another. He specially supervises our purification.

At the same time, notice that "**He will sit as a refiner**." The *sitting* posture shows that the Refiner may seem indifferent, but He is not. He is carefully working with the silver, burning off and scraping away the dross that the flames bring to the top. Sitting seems to imply that it is hard and continual work that needs special concentration. It will take care and constant attention. God loves us so much that He will never turn up the heat and walk away.

If you find yourself in the fire right now, be encouraged from this passage. The mere fact that you are in the fire shows that you are indeed *silver*, that you are *precious* to God, that you are capable of being *more pure* and suited to His service, and that He gives you special attention as the fires purify you.

Malachi has strong criticism against the priests of his day, but also has this encouraging promise: "**He will purify the sons of Levi**." In the early chapters of Malachi, the LORD spoke out against the corruption of the priests. Here, God gave His ultimate answer for that corruption - the Messiah "**will purify the sons of Levi**." He will do it and it will get done.

We draw special comfort from the idea that when the refining work of Jesus is done upon us, there will never be a need for it again. There are no purifying fires in the life to come, so we take greater courage in the Refiner's fire that we face today. Most of all, we find rest in the special attention with which He supervises our purification.

SEVENTY
Bible Reading: Malachi 4

THE SUN OF RIGHTEOUSNESS

*"But to you who fear My name the Sun of Righteousness shall arise
with healing in His wings; and you shall go out and grow fat like
stall-fed calves. You shall trample the wicked, for they shall be ashes
under the soles of your feet on the day that I do this," says the LORD of
hosts.* (Malachi 4:2-3)

In the first verse of Malachi 4, God promised a judgment of fire
for the *proud*. That is what we should expect, because the proud do
not think they need God but tend to trust in their own abilities. Yet
God says, those "**Who fear My name**" will be saved.

They will be saved because something wonderful is promised:
"**The Sun of Righteousness shall arise**." From the time of early
Christians like Justin Martyr to today, Christians have regarded the
Sun of Righteousness as a reference to Jesus. In many passages God
is related to a planet or star (Psalm 84:11, Isaiah 60:19, Revelation
22:16, Numbers 24:17). Here, the Messiah is not only a **Sun**, but
also the **Sun of Righteousness** who brings **healing**. He is both a
Son and a **Sun**, shining brightly in all His glory.

If we meditate a bit on this picture, we can think of Jesus going
under a cloud when He suffered in His passion; but then breaking
forth and rising like the bright **Sun of Righteousness**, gleaming
with His beams of glory at the resurrection.

The idea of "beams of glory" is suggested by Malachi when he
describes the Messiah as coming forth "**with healing in His wings**."
In the thinking of the ancient mind, the **wings** of the sun are the rays
or sunbeams it sends out. They bring healing, joy, and wholeness.
When the **Sun of Righteousness** shines, we need no other light or
warmth. Imagine lighting a candle on a sunny day to brighten up

the day when the sun is shining in full strength! It is just as foolish to think we can improve on the work of Jesus by our own righteousness.

This shining **Sun of Righteousness** not only brings healing, it also brings joy and victory: "**You shall trample the wicked**." When God's people see the final resolution of all things they will be so happy they will jump about like **stall-fed calves** that are set free from the pen. As they jump about with joy, the **wicked** are trampled beneath their feet.

Do you see the word picture that Malachi used? Think of a calf in a stall in a barn, tied up in the stall through the night. But when the sun rises, the calf is set free and goes out to the pasture. Even so, the child of God may be in a dark season of bondage – the remembrance of past sins and present unbelief may tie him up and keep him confined in the stall. But when the LORD shines forth as the **Sun of Righteousness**, He brings healing, liberty, and victory.

We can see a glorious progression in those who look upon the risen **Sun of Righteousness** and receive the **healing in His wings**:

• They **shall go out** - they will be free and enjoy their liberty.

• They shall **grow fat** - growing strong and prosperous in the LORD.

• They shall **trample the wicked** - enjoying the LORD's victory in their life.

Perhaps it isn't best to say that it is time to rise and shine; instead it is time to rise and let the **Sun of Righteousness** shine upon you. As you hear the voice of God speaking through the Minor Prophets, you can stay *near to God and be true to Him.*

Great thanks to those who helped with this book. Inga-Lill offered some excellent suggestions and Craig Brewer helped design the cover, as well as providing the cover photo. Special thanks to those who contributed but didn't want to be named (again).

David Guzik's Bible commentary is regularly used and trusted by many thousands who want to know the Bible better. Pastors, teachers, class leaders, and everyday Christians find his commentary helpful for their own understanding and explanation of the Bible. David and his wife Inga-Lill live in Santa Barbara, California.

You can email David at
david@enduringword.com

For more resources by David Guzik,
go to www.enduringword.com

CPSIA information can be obtained
at www.ICGtesting.com
Printed in the USA
FSHW020103160120

9 781565 990326